My Child My Chance

Guarding and Guiding Your Child's Identity in the Chaos of Culture and Sex Education

Susan Zuidema
with Charlotte Goulding

MY CHILD, MY CHANCE: Guarding and Guiding Your Child's Identity in the Chaos of Culture and Sex Education

All Scripture quotations are taken from the Holy Bible, New international Version ®, NIV (unless otherwise noted). Copyright © 1973, 1978, 1984, 2011 by Biblica Inc.™
Italics in Scripture quotations reflect the author's added emphasis.

Copyright ©2017 by Susan Zuidema and Charlotte Goulding
Cover design by Jana Johnson, The Paint and Pixel Design Company, www.ppdco.com

All rights reserved. No portion of this book may be reproduced, stored in a retrieval system, or transmitted in any form or by any means – electronic, mechanical, photocopy, recording, scanning, or other – except for brief quotations in critical reviews or articles, without the prior written permission of the authors.

Paperback ISBN 978-0-9959032-0-3
eBook ISBN 978-0-9959032-1-0

My Child, My Chance
Brantford, Ontario
Susan C. Zuidema, 1973-
Charlotte Goulding, 1980-

For more information, please email info@mychildmychance.com or visit www.mychildmychance.com.

Wake up Sleeper,

Rise from the dead,

and Christ will shine on you.

Be very careful, then, how you live—

not as unwise but as wise,

making the most of every opportunity,

because the days are evil.

Ephesians 5:14-16

Acknowledgements

From Sue's heart ...

First, I thank my husband, Alan, whose unconditional, unwavering support freed me up to research and write. Your honest opinion and ideas kept me focused along the way. I love you and I couldn't have gotten this far without you.

Char and Kim – your friendships are God's gift to me out of this project. I love you both so much! Kim, your company on writing weekends, belief in me, and in the urgency of this topic kept me going. Your patience when I had to set aside *Created for a Purpose* to get this project finished first – thanks for being so understanding.

Char, you came along at the right time to encourage and share the load with editing, writing, and researching ... not to mention your knowledge of the whole medical side of things. Your sense of humour kept me from total despair at dark times in the process and your attention to detail sometimes drove me crazy. Thank you.

Mom and Dad, your support has been constant. I know how truly shocked you'll be if this book does not sell ten thousand copies and win awards. You've invested in every possible way and have prayed constantly, which I appreciate most of all. Thanks.

Many other friends – new and old – stepped up along the way. Thank you to Phil Lees and his team from PEACE Ontario for our many conversations, meetings, and your prayer and support; Peter Jon Mitchell of CARDUS Canada for sharing resources and your mentorship at key points along the way; Rick Hiemstra of the Evangelical Fellowship of Canada whose conversations and emails provided a whole new perspective; Tami Chism Stevenson, the Grammar Queen, for her advice and help with some tricky editing; Jana Johnson for her inspired work on our cover; and lastly the group of friends who gave financially at a key point in the project.

Finally, I thank *you*, Lord Jesus, for laying this on my heart and trusting me with it. So many times I have thought of the stronger, wiser people you could have chosen – often wishing that you had – and yet here I am, almost two years into this project, finishing up with many tears, fears, and trembling. I can only pray that you will continue to move in your invisible, wise ways to use this clumsy effort as you have planned. I am so thankful for the message of your Holy Word which is fresh and relevant no matter what the culture, always having everything I need, just when I need it.

From Char's heart ...

I would like to thank first and foremost my Lord and Saviour Jesus Christ. You were so patient with me as I tiptoed and eventually jumped out of that boat, into your sea of grace.

Sue, little did I know that phone call from a stranger at 9:00 am on a Saturday morning would be the start of an amazing partnership and friendship that I will cherish for the rest of my life. Through this process, God has used you to reveal his purposes for me, and has opened my mind and heart to my true identity in him. I can never thank you enough for that. Kim, you are a powerhouse! Your enthusiasm and mama's heart have been so encouraging. Thank you.

Corey, I am blessed beyond words to share this life with you. You are the greatest example of God's grace to me. Your intellect and wisdom have been a terrific sounding board for ideas in this book. To my kids, thank you for your unwavering support and interest in "Sue's book." You are seriously, for real, the best kids in the world.

To my family and friends, who have put their prayers and financial support behind Sue and I, thank-you so much. And lastly, Mom and Dad, you gave me the greatest gift of all by raising me to know and love Jesus, and for that, I will truly be eternally grateful.

*We dedicate this book to our children.
May you never doubt that God made you a masterpiece,
that your life is full of purpose, and his incredible
design and plans for you are so, so good.
When we look at you, we see his fingerprints.*

TABLE OF CONTENTS

Before We Begin 13

Part 1 ~ THE CHAOS OF CULTURE
Exchanging the Truth For a Lie

From Tolerance To Acceptance And Respect 25
The Cultural Shift 41
Our True Identity in the Chaos of Sexuality 63
Our True Identity in the Chaos of Gender 79
Religious Freedom: The Lesser of Human Rights 105

Part 2 ~ THE CHAOS OF SEX EDUCATION
When Children Are Taught To Accept a Lie

The Culture Comes to the Classroom 123
Unbuckling the Gender Straightjacket 137
Love Who You Want to Love 153
Tossing Out the Trash 165
The Silence is Deafening 179
It's All About Me 201

Appendix 215
Bibliography 221
Glossary 235
Index 239

A Note to the Reader

This book was written in response to the Health and Physical Education Curriculum (the curriculum) that was released in 2015 in Ontario, Canada. The curriculum covers graphic sexual and human rights education which the government pushed forward in spite of substantial parental backlash. This curriculum exposed what was already there but hidden within the culture and the schools: a push for sexual freedom and self-defined sexual identity for our children.

The Ontario curriculum is based on comprehensive sex education (CSE). CSE was developed by the International Planned Parenthood Federation, and endorsed by the United Nations and the World Health Organization. With this substantial support system, CSE has been gaining momentum worldwide and is now found in many countries.[1]

With that being said, perhaps something similar is being taught openly in your region or maybe it is still hidden. Be assured … it is there. I encourage you to investigate your local curriculum and the classroom practices in your district to see how they line up to what is covered in Ontario and in CSE.

Generally, examples and many of the terms in this book are from the Ontario curriculum. Key terms that may need clarification are shown in bold. These are included in the **glossary** so you can fully understand the terms as I am using them.

---

[1] Phil Lees, "Sex Ed and Public Schools – Ontario: Guiding through the Sex Ed Confusion" (PEACE Ontario, 2015), http://peaceontario.com/wp-content/uploads/2015/01/PEACE-Sex-Ed-Report-2015.pdf.

BEFORE WE BEGIN

In June 2016, newsfeeds everywhere filled with reports of the largest mass shooting in American history. Forty-nine dead, and fifty-three wounded in an attack on a gay club in Orlando. Justifiably, our culture is screaming against the hate that provokes this kind of unthinkable devastation.

The shooting and the motivation of hate is heartbreaking. As Christians, we grieve with the rest of society. We know that as God's hands and feet we need to do much better. What is the answer? How should we treat people who identify as lesbian, gay, bisexual or transgendered (LGBT)?[a]

I believe the answer is simple. We need to show love. Everyone is greatly loved by God and we need to embrace all people with love just as he does. Jesus modelled how to love without accepting sin, in the story of the woman caught in adultery.[b] Instead of slapping others with hateful and hurtful words, he taught us to turn the other cheek.[c] The ideals to which Christians strive do not leave room for hateful thoughts, words or actions.

And yet, sometimes Christians act as though there is an exception whereby we can treat the LGBT community with hostility or bias. If this has been your outlook or you have seen this modelled in your church or friendships, you need to recognize and reject that sinful attitude. All people are created in God's image and deserve respect

---

[a] Throughout this book we use the acronym "LGBT" in lieu of other variations, except in the context of a direct quote. Adding letters such as Q (for Queer or Questioning) may be an attempt to categorize those who don't fit neatly under the LGBT banner however, we are concerned about inaccurately grouping those who may be confused about their identity with those who have adopted an LGBT identity.
[b] John 8:1-11
[c] Matthew 5:39

and love. "For God so loved the world [*not excluding anyone!*] that He gave His only begotten Son ..."[d] The Bible is clear. All people are equally worthy of God's love; Jesus came and died for everyone. There are no exceptions or exclusions.

In contrast to hate or homophobia, we are instructed to be gentle and humble toward others.

- "Let your gentleness be evident to all, the Lord is near."[e]
- "Do nothing out of selfish ambition or vain conceit. Rather, in humility value others above yourselves."[f]
- "But the fruit of the Spirit is love, joy, peace, forbearance, kindness, goodness, faithfulness, gentleness, and self-control. Against such things there is no law."[g]

If God's example of love was not enough, we are also commanded to love our neighbour as ourselves, and that includes the LGBT community.[h] We can do no less than tangibly show that love when we interact with those who are LGBT.

Christians, by and large, have not been known for love toward the LGBT community but rather for pointing fingers. Some of us have been bitter, judgmental, and condemning as the demands to accept LGBT practices have grown. The truth is, we haven't had the answers. We know we can't accept the sin so how do we respond to those who engage in it or even flaunt it? The questions are tough and I have wrestled with them as people dear to me have adopted an LGBT identity. In our conversations, I have tried to speak both truth and love but I know I have often failed.

As a culture, we have come to believe that love and relationships are primarily based on romantic and sexual attraction, and so some

---

[d] John 3:16a
[e] Philippians 4:5
[f] Philippians 2:3
[g] Galatians 5:22-23
[h] Mark 12:31

have been quick to pardon, support, or even adopt a lesbian, gay, or bisexual identity. As we explore this in the chapters ahead, we will discover that rejecting the identity God has given us in order to adopt an identity based on sin (because we can't hang onto both!) brings us great physical, emotional, and spiritual harm.

God created each one of us for a specific purpose. This is true for every person who ever lived on this earth. He has delighted in each one from before time began,[i] designing and equipping them uniquely[j] for a life of purpose and fulfillment.[k]

All people were created in the image of God, born with the capacity to bring him glory and honour. The tragedy is when the enemy succeeds in getting people to believe a lie that affects their identity at its core. God does not make mistakes and the good news is that brokenness or lies do not need to have the final word in anyone's life.

This introduction does not allow for all the questions and answers Christians have about LGBT identities. My hope is that some of the answers might be supplied as you read this book. If there are times when you are reading that you feel offended, hurt, or angered, please know that I have prayed and wrestled with my words in order to balance truth with love.

My intent is not to hurt or speak hate. My desire is to help other believers navigate these issues, particularly when they arise in the school system so that we can honour God and our purpose as his hands and feet in our culture and in our families.

---

[i] Ephesians 1:4
[j] 2 Peter 1:3
[k] John 10:10

Wake Up!

A bit of backstory about how I came to the place of researching and writing this book. As you'll see, the process has been about as subtle as a wrecking ball.

Wake-Up Call #1

In early 2015, the Ontario government released its new sexual education curriculum. Concerns over its graphic content set off immense parental backlash. As an elementary school teacher and a Christian, I started analyzing the curriculum and the topics parents were objecting to. I began to get concerned.

Wake-Up Call #2

Not long after, I sat and listened intently as a young friend chatted on about life in grade eleven in a public high school. As a matter of course in the conversation, several statements quickly caught my attention.

"He hangs out with the gay crowd."

"Well, she's pansexual ..."

"This guy kissed him and he was all disgusted, but he says he's not homophobic."

I couldn't believe what I was hearing. Was this life in high school? When did this become normal? I looked at my husband and made the understatement of the year: "Things have sure changed since we were teenagers!"

Wake-Up Call #3

I posted an article on social media entitled, "Forcing a Girl to Share a Bathroom With a Gender-confused Boy is Abuse."[1] In the post, I expressed concern over the safety of young women due to gender-neutral bathroom policies. A seventeen-year-old girl responded, "Protection of young women? I am a 'young woman' and if someone wanted to change their identity to the opposite sex the LAST thing I would feel is unprotected, especially in the change room."

She went on, "If you're saying that boys who are straight could pretend to be transgender just to look at the girls that's totally a possibility but what if you're wrong?" As the exchange continued, it became clear that the possibility of hurting or offending someone who claims to be transgendered would trump her concern for her own safety.

These personal moments were sharpened by articles on my news feed. This took me on a journey where I learned the many ways our culture has shifted to accept progressively extreme forms of sexuality and expression.

I share these moments for one purpose: To Wake You Up. If you are, like I was, blissfully unaware of how the next generation has totally bought into sexual freedom and gender diversity, you need to realize that it's happening. As believers, we have been blind to the fact that our kids are starting to support, or even champion, lifestyles or choices that we can't even label. And *we* are now the backward ones. *We* are intolerant and hateful. *We* are called homophobic by our own children.

This *Vanity Fair* cover showcasing former Olympian Bruce Jenner in his new gender identity as Caitlyn embodies the breakneck transition happening in our culture.

How did this happen? Where were the warning signs? And more importantly, how can we reclaim our children? We need a plan to reinforce the foundation beneath them so they can stand firm in the identity given to them by their Creator God. Our children's faith needs to be resilient against the cultural forces that have the power to cause them confusion and end in grief.

Mitigating the Risks

A major force impacting our children's mindset and development is their experience at school. In Ontario, Canada, the health and physical education curriculum which deals with sexual development is a mixed bag. On the one hand, it contains some helpful information, but some pieces may be harmful or misleading, and some are even missing. What is most troubling is that it contains ideas that could dramatically affect a child's understanding of his or her identity.

The enemy's attack is levelled at the source of our children's identity, that is, who they believe themselves to be.

We live in a country in which there are many options for schooling our children. Most of us put our children in the free public school system. Others choose private Christian education or homeschool their kids. However, there are many families concerned about the direction of public education for whom Christian education or homeschooling will not work. Still others, knowing what they are up against, choose public school in order to be "salt and light" in their neighbourhood. The question for all these families is: how can we raise our kids to have a faith that is intact, grounded, and strong?

As I prayed through this question, I realized that the enemy's attack in public education and the culture is levelled at the source of our children's identity, that is, who they believe themselves to be. It is crucial that parents recognize this because then we can become equipped to address the problem. If this concern resonates with you, please do not give up hope. It is our firm belief that this battle can be won. But we have to engage. If our children do not find opposition to Christian beliefs at school, they will find it in the playground or sports arena, and most definitely in the media and online.

The goal for this book is to educate and equip families who want to raise their children to believe and respect God's Word. I also hope to appeal to other faiths and even families with no faith background who are concerned about current trends regarding sex and gender. We've met self-proclaimed atheists who are frustrated that they are expected to raise their boys and girls in a so-called genderless society. This is especially tough to do when traditional and biblical values are portrayed as old-fashioned and counter-culture, or even bigoted and hateful. However, we are confident in the truth of God's Word and the power of his Holy Spirit working through us.

After you have read this resource, I hope you will feel challenged and ready to take on the task of guarding and guiding your children as they encounter their culture. Our companion discipleship series, *Created for a Purpose*, due for release later in 2017, is another resource to equip you for the task. It contains detailed lessons designed to help you speak truth to your children about who they are in Christ. These lessons will prepare your children for the confusing messages from the media, the culture, and the classroom. They will see that they were created to fulfill a unique purpose. Their identity will be grounded in the knowledge that they are sons and daughters of God, and they will understand that their identity is not tied up in their sexuality or gender. It is my prayer that your children will have an impact on their classrooms and the lives of those around them – those who have bought the lie that their identity is found in their sexuality or gender.

A Word About Compromise

Watching and listening to parents around me, it's clear there are many responses to the problems that comprehensive sex education such as the Ontario health curriculum poses. What has been the response to sex education in your province or state? In Ontario, some parents have been fighting through social media, rallies, surveys, letters, and meetings with government officials. Some are taking matters into their own hands by withdrawing their children from the public system and choosing home or private school.

Some parents choose compromise, buckling to cultural pressure or simply giving in to their own preferences. Compromise is trying to squish an obviously square peg into the round hole that is the Bible.

This book is not for those who would compromise because this is not an option for those who want to honour God. The reason for this is that God does not change.[l] Change is not in his nature because change assumes a mistake has been made and God does not make mistakes. "God is not human, that he should lie, not a human being, that he should change his mind. Does he speak and then not act? Does he promise and not fulfill?"[m] What God has spoken in his Word will never change. He is a "majority of one" and we, his creation, cannot vote him down.

Finally, many others are very concerned but have no idea what can be done about it! Maybe you belong to this group and that's why you have chosen to read this book. Don't worry, Charlotte and I have both been there, and we are thrilled you have decided to partner with us as we share what we've learned. What we can do is cling to His promise that "joyful are those who obey his laws and search for him with all their hearts. They do not compromise with evil, and they walk only in his paths."[n] This is the opposite of how the culture tells us we will feel if we do not compromise. Those who hold fast to God's standards for sex are seen as joyless, uptight, and stoic. Not so. "Joyful!" God promises. I trust in that and have seen its evidence in my own life. I have also experienced the painful consequences of compromise but through his grace, I carry on.

---

[l] Malachi 3:6a
[m] Numbers 23:19
[n] Psalm 119:2-3, NLT

In the midst of whatever else we are doing in response to change in the culture, *we need to accept a wake-up call.* Remaining passive about our God-given responsibility to disciple our kids will mean a dramatic decline of Christianity in our culture in their generation. It's that simple.

Are you awake? Let's get started!

---

[1] Matt Walsh, "Forcing Girls To Share A Bathroom With A Gender-Confused Boy Is Abuse," *The Blaze,* September 2, 2015, accessed September 3, 2015, http://www.theblaze.com/contributions/forcing-girls-to-share-a-bathroom-with-a-gender-confused-boy-is-abuse/.

Magazine highlighted in this chapter:
Buzz Bissinger, photo by Annie Leibovitz, "Call Me Caitlyn," *Vanity Fair*, July, 2015.

Part 1

THE CHAOS OF CULTURE:

EXCHANGING THE TRUTH FOR A LIE

"They exchanged the truth about God for a lie, and worshiped and served created things rather than the Creator."

Romans 1:25

Chapter 1

FROM TOLERANCE
TO ACCEPTANCE AND RESPECT

*"Do not conform to the pattern of this world,
but be transformed by the renewing of your mind."*

Romans 12:2a

If you want to know what kids are hearing and believing about their sexuality, you can start by reading this. It's from a website that the Toronto District School Board says contains "interesting facts" and "teaching and learning strategies"[1] that may be useful for its schools.

> If you think you might be queer, relax! Everyone has questions about their sexuality at some time or other, and exploring your sexual feelings is important and exciting. If you're not sure if you're bisexual, lesbian, straight, transgender, or gay, just stay tuned to your sexual feelings and see what they tell you. You don't even have to decide on a label to call yourself. You can make up

your own name for your sexuality. Your sexuality is totally unique to you, and it's yours to ENJOY, not to worry about![2]

This rather casual invitation to explore sexuality makes the experience sound exciting and risk-free. Although "straight" is listed, it gets lost among the LGBT identities: **lesbian, gay, bisexual** and **transgender.** What the website fails to mention, here or elsewhere, is that those who identify as LGBT are at high risk. People who are LGBT have higher rates of:

- Depression
- Anxiety
- Obsessive-compulsive disorders
- Self-harm and substance use
- Suicidal thoughts
- Childhood sexual experiences
- Serious psychiatric disorders
- Illegal drug use. About twice as many LGBT individuals use cocaine and other illegal drugs.
- Death by suicide. For men who have sex with men the rate of suicide is as high as, or higher than the number of deaths by HIV.[3]

There's no doubt that emotional support is needed for people who struggle with their sexuality or gender. But what does this support look like? The push is to eliminate "misconceptions" and "erroneous information"[4] about gender identity and **sexual orientation** through education. Much has been made about the role of **homophobia**, and more recently **transphobia** – terms that suggest those with traditional values are fearful, ignorant, and even hateful towards those in the LGBT community.

The risk factors above are serious and are always cited as a driving reason to improve anti-homophobia education. Strangely though, in the most accepting, pro-homosexual communities in the world, problems such as high suicide rates persist even when homophobia is no longer a significant factor.[5] Even though mental health challenges may be heightened due to rejection by family, friends or the culture at large, it's clear that homophobia is not the only factor.

At the risk of making a sweeping statement, let's acknowledge that a person with same-sex attraction is a person in some emotional pain. In reading case studies and listening to the stories of people who experience same-sex attraction or gender dysphoria, we hear a common refrain of brokenness – abuse, neglect, pornography addictions. While it wouldn't be fair to say that each person who struggles in this way automatically has this kind of backstory, we can't ignore the fact that many, sadly, do. As a result, it is difficult to believe that all these mental health challenges have their source in homophobia, and we must consider the possibility that there is unresolved brokenness that needs healing.

Like the culture around us, we acknowledge the pain. But what is the solution? The culture's suggestion is that these individuals embrace the brokenness, the LGBT identity. However, the truth is that taking on this identity will ultimately produce even more emotional and spiritual brokenness (not to mention the potential physical harm of LGBT practices – more on this in chapter 11). Here, we will examine the LGBT rights movement and how it has led to the unfolding of comprehensive sex education in Canadian schools.

Gay and Transgender Rights

As late as 1965, people engaging in a homosexual act were charged as "dangerous sexual offenders" and punished by imprisonment, even in situations of consensual sex – obviously not the right response. Fast forward five decades and homosexuality and transgenderism are publicly celebrated and protected as a human right.

Let's consider how this happened. Although slow to gain momentum, change did come. Studying the steps and stages between the complete turn-about from 1965 to present day, will help us recognize how important it is to be socially aware and involved.

1948 The Kinsey report (later proven as deeply flawed[6]) states 10% of the population is gay, lesbian, or bisexual. This figure has gone unchallenged for over half a century.

1965 Everett Klippert is imprisoned indefinitely as a "dangerous sexual offender" for "admitting he was gay and that he had sex with other men" and was unlikely to change.[7]

1969 Canadian Prime Minister Pierre Trudeau decriminalizes homosexuality.

1977 Quebec becomes the first province in Canada to include sexual orientation in its Human Rights Code.

1980-1992 Bills to increase the rights of homosexuals fail, including attempts to add "sexual orientation" to the Canadian Human Rights Act and changing the definition of spouse in the Income Tax/Canada Pension Plan Acts to include same-sex couples.

1992 Gays and lesbians are no longer banned from the military.

1995 Same-sex couples can legally adopt their partner's children.

1996 "Sexual orientation" is added to Canadian Human Rights Act.

2000 "Policy on Discrimination and Harassment Because Of Sexual Orientation" is approved by the Ontario Human Rights Commission. Sexual orientation is recognized as "an immutable personal characteristic that forms part of an individual's core identity."[8]

	New legislation gives same-sex couples the same social and tax benefits as heterosexuals in common-law relationships. Marriage remains defined as "the lawful union of one man and one woman to the exclusion of all others."[9]
2003-2005	Ontario becomes the first province to legalize same-sex marriage, followed by British Columbia, Quebec, Manitoba Nova Scotia, Newfoundland Labrador, and New Brunswick.
2005	Canada becomes the fourth country in the world to officially recognize same-sex marriage.
2012	"Gender identity" and "gender expression" are added to the *Ontario Human Rights Code*.[10]
2015	Statistics Canada reports that 3% of Canadians aged 18-59 said they are gay, lesbian, or bisexual[11] (7% lower than the 1948 Kinsey Report).
2015	Graduates from a proposed law school at Trinity Western University (British Columbia) are denied the ability to practice law in various Canadian provinces. This is because of Trinity's code of conduct that holds students to a high level of sexual morality (refraining from homosexual sex, as well as pre-marital heterosexual sex). Decisions are appealed and Ontario's Supreme Court upholds the ruling that Trinity Western is acting in a discriminatory manner; British Columbia's and Nova Scotia's Supreme Courts overrule the decision.[12]
2015	Gay marriage is legalized in the United States.

It's not over. As I write, Bill C-16 has passed and is in second reading in the Canadian Senate. This bill adds gender identity and gender expression as grounds for discrimination to the Canadian Human Rights Act. Updates to provincial human rights codes have already been used to accuse people of hate speech when they have refused to use pronouns such as "zhe or zir" and to rationalize giving transgendered persons access to gender-specific public bathrooms.

Human Rights

Rights for those who identify as LGBT are protected across Canada. Manitoba and the Northwest Territories protect the grounds of "gender identity" while Nova Scotia also includes "gender expression." In provinces and territories without these provisions, discrimination because of gender identity is addressed under the ground of "sex."[13] The Canadian government is attempting to eliminate the perception of ambiguity by the changes proposed in Bill C-16.[14]

We do not argue against anyone's right to be free from discrimination. Like all Canadians, a person who identifies as LGBT should have an opportunity "to make for themselves the lives that they are able and wish to have and to have their needs accommodated, consistent with their duties and obligations as members of society, without being hindered in or prevented from doing so by discriminatory practices."[15] But what happens when one ground for discrimination conflicts with another?

The Ontario's Human Rights Code (the Code) aims to "recognize the dignity and worth of every person and to provide for equal rights and opportunities without discrimination."[16] The Code also guarantees "the right to education, community and other services that respect your sincerely held religious practices and beliefs."[17] However, schools argue that they "have a legal duty to provide students with an education environment free from harassment and other forms of discrimination because of Code grounds."[18]

There's a tension here that can't be avoided because some specific Code grounds are based on practices which are prohibited by a number of religions. This does not mean that people of those religions would or should in any way harass people who identify under those grounds. Clearly that type of behaviour would also contradict many faiths' values. Yet there's no denying that it causes conflict when children are instructed to accept practices which violate their faith or to consider them as equal, appropriate options.

In Ontario, the Code set the ball in motion for what is now happening in schools. Take a look.

2000   Sexual orientation is added to the Ontario Human Rights Code.

2006   In the province's *Language* curriculum update, diversity encompasses "gender, race, culture, ethnicity, sexual orientation, ability/disability, age, religion, and socio-economic level."[19]

2009   In the *Arts* curriculum update, students explore issues related to their self-identity and gender stereotyping. Discrimination now includes racism, sexism, homophobia, and religious intolerance.[20]

2010   An update to the *Health and Physical Education* curriculum is released. It is withdrawn within days due to intense parental backlash over the sexual health education, and sexual and gender diversity elements which parents declared age inappropriate and radical.

2011   A Toronto District School Board (TDSB) curriculum supplement entitled *Challenging Homophobia and Heterosexism* is released. It seeks to implement many of the elements that were a part of the rejected 2010 curriculum stating that, "[TDSB] is committed to enabling all ... LGBTQ students ... to see themselves reflected in the curriculum."[21] This resource is made freely available province-wide to enable this purpose.

2012   Gender diversity and expression are added to the Code. Following this, the *Ontario Education Act* is amended by

> *The Accepting Schools Act* (Bill 13) to address bullying based on sexual orientation, gender identity, and gender expression, saying that these individuals are more vulnerable to "discrimination, harassment, violence, and suicide."[22] This bill requires schools to "provide support to students who have engaged in inappropriate behaviour or been affected by inappropriate behaviour."[23]
>
> Also in 2012, the Ontario Ministry of Education published "Policy/Program Memorandum 145: Progressive Discipline and Promoting Positive Student Behaviour" outlining how discipline should be handled for "bullying, swearing, homophobic or racial slurs, sexist comments or jokes, graffiti, or vandalism."[24]

2013 In the *Social Studies* curriculum update, diversity includes "ancestry, culture, ethnicity, gender identity, language, physical and intellectual ability, race, religion, sex, sexual orientation, and socio-economic status."[25] Sample families considered in grade two include same-sex families[26] and in grade six, the legalization of gay marriage is given as an example for assessing the inclusiveness of Canada.[27]

2015 A new *Health and Physical Education* curriculum update is rolled out. It is nearly identical to the 2010 curriculum that was rejected by parents, except in areas where it takes the ideology further. Parental response is once again overwhelming and negative but this time, the curriculum remains. Gender identity and expression, and sexual orientation are included throughout in an overarching human rights theme.

The transition toward human rights education has not happened overnight and it should be pointed out that it has not been driven specifically by the education system. Rather, it has followed changes in the culture.

When Tolerance is Not Tolerated

The reaction to Ontario's curriculum made national headlines in both its 2010 and 2015 releases. In spite of parental concern and commitment to action, the curriculum has not been pulled. If you are from another part of the country, you may not have heard much about updates to the curriculum in your area. But don't be fooled: the curriculum follows the culture. Even if our schools' curriculums were somehow retracted or watered down, we need to face the fact that the culture is heavily weighted in favour of free sexual expression, and this includes the right to any sexual orientation and gender identity that suits a particular individual.

I recently sat in a professional activity day workshop organized by the local teacher's union. The agenda was mental health awareness but the first thirty minutes were spent talking about LGBT rights and introducing a video resource that had been sent to each school for use at a future staff meeting. The first few segments were shown to the group of over a thousand teachers.

In the video, a clip was shown of a lesbian principal who talked about her experience starting at a new school. She shared being impressed to see several motivational posters around the school about inclusivity and respect but being troubled by a poster that spoke of tolerance for LGBT individuals. She said she had to take it down. In her words, tolerance was no longer acceptable because who wants to just be tolerated? She said what she wants is acceptance and respect.

Of course, no one wants to just be "tolerated" as an individual or put up with reluctantly; we all want to be accepted. I absolutely get that. As we pointed out in, "Before We Begin," Christians should be accepting and loving toward all people. However, we need to be careful to draw a distinction between accepting and loving the person, and affirming sinful practices as morally acceptable.

It is this type of acceptance – considering LGBT practices to be morally sound and no different from heterosexual ones – that is the motive behind the curriculum, and various legislation and school board policies. It stems from the mandate of *Ontario's Equity and Inclusive Education Strategy* where the goal of *"moving beyond tolerance to acceptance and respect"*[28] of sexual and gender diversity is clearly stated.

As humans, we crave acceptance and Christians should be the first to show it. With our example – Jesus, friend of sinners – how can we do any less? So I challenge you. The *person* – we can, and must, accept and love. The *practice* – we simply can't. As we explore this further, let's bear in mind this tension between grace (loving and accepting the person) and truth (recognizing the practice as sin).[a][29]

So can Christians do this? Accept means "to regard as sound or true; to believe; to accept a claim."[30] As believers, we cannot accept homosexuality or transgenderism as human qualities that are morally sound, helpful, or true. Instead, we need to instruct our children in gentleness and forbearance – in the art of agreeing to disagree – but we need to make a clear distinction between tolerance and acceptance. We *tolerate* the practice. We *accept* the person.

Parents need to be aware. The schools have incredible influence over the next generation: the development of their thoughts, beliefs, and ideology. When beliefs like those outlined in the curriculum are mandated by the unions and the school boards, and then taught by a child's teacher, parents need to have a plan.

---

[a] For more on the tension between grace and truth, I highly recommend Caleb Kaltenbach's book, *Messy Grace*, (Colorado Springs: Water Brook Press, 2015).

Are Christians Homophobic?

Homophobia is defined by the curriculum as "a disparaging or hostile attitude or a negative bias, which may be overt or unspoken and which may exist at an individual and/or a systemic level, towards people who are lesbian, gay, bisexual, or transgender (LGBT)."[31] Simplified, the core of the definition is hostility or negativity expressed in any way toward people who are LGBT.

After speaking at a workshop on the topic of this book, I was approached by a grade twelve student. She shared her struggles as a Christian high school student, and her question was, "How can I relate to others who identify as gay or lesbian? As a Christian, I'm always being called homophobic!"

She's not alone. I believe many Christians would reject being called homophobic but aren't sure how to respond to the term. What is the attitude of the believer to be toward others, specifically those whose expression of sexuality or identity opposes our religious beliefs about what is good and helpful … or sinful?

For me, it boils down to the old precept which is biblical in its roots: "I don't care how much you know, until I know how much you care." Ephesians 4:15 reminds us about "speaking the truth in love." 1 John 3:18 takes this idea even further, urging us not to "love with words or speech but with actions and in truth." How profound! John is saying, "Don't walk around telling others that you love them. Show them! If it's really true, there should be no question about your love." Peter also has much to say about how we should interact with unbelievers.

> Always be prepared to give an answer to everyone who asks you to give the reason for the hope that you have. But do this with gentleness and respect, keeping a clear conscience, so that those who

speak maliciously against your good behavior in Christ may be ashamed of their slander.[b]

Above all, love each other deeply, because love covers over a multitude of sins. Offer hospitality to one another without grumbling. Each of you should use whatever gift you have received to serve others, as faithful stewards of God's grace in its various forms. If anyone speaks, they should do so as one who speaks the very words of God.[c]

Bearing all this in mind, I believe we can follow these guidelines when working with or talking to people who are actively engaging in sinful behaviour:

1. *Do* continually communicate love toward all people following God's example as shared by Jesus in John 3:16. No one is going to be won over by your arguments, no matter how well researched or persuasive you are. People will, however, be won over by your love.

2. *Do* make sure you separate what someone does from who they are. It is much more beneficial to caution or challenge someone's *behaviour* or *thinking* without judging them as a person.

3. Keeping points #1 and #2 in mind, *don't* speak about someone's behaviour or thinking unless:

    a) someone's safety (including his/her own) is compromised by reckless choices or lifestyle *or*

    b) you are sought out and your opinion or help is asked for by the person *or*

    c) you are in a close relationship with that person. But let me be clear, he or she must first have no doubt of your love because of your past kindness. I believe that then,

---

[b] 1 Peter 3:15b-16
[c] 1 Peter 4:11a

and only then, can you lovingly communicate concern for that individual's spiritual well-being and lead him or her to truth.

When you do have the opportunity or the need to speak about the consequences of choosing to identify with or live in sin, you need to be well informed. It's a good start to know what the Bible says about identity, sin, and forgiveness. Current curriculum, strategies, and policies of the public school system are such that students will be distanced from their true identity in Christ while deepening their identification with sin. With that in mind, it's the goal of this book to equip you with this kind of biblical background so that you are able to speak knowledgeably and lovingly in these situations.

As a final note, I want to go back to the conversation I had with the young woman who was discouraged by being labelled homophobic. The truth is, we are all afraid of that. But as Char pointed out during that conversation, Jesus warns us that we will be hated because of our faith in him.[d] Interestingly, in the same passage quoted previously, Peter gives a similar warning and it is so pertinent to the issue of homophobia.

> For you have spent enough time in the past doing what pagans choose to do — living in debauchery, lust, drunkenness, orgies, carousing and detestable idolatry. They are surprised that you do not join them in their reckless, wild living, and they heap abuse on you.[e]

Notice how the unbelievers in Peter's day are confused about why believers do not engage or approve of sinful behaviour. Their confusion led them to heaping abuse on the believers. It's the same today. All around us are people who cannot understand why on

---

[d] Matthew 10:22
[e] 1 Peter 4:3, 4

earth we object to homosexuality and gender diversity, and we are instantly labelled homophobic (or worse) for doing so.

It is important to note that as careful as we may be with our thoughts, words, and actions, there will always be a person or group who is ready to pounce on every word we say.

This is our reality. It is the cross we bear with Jesus.

Peter says we are to rejoice when we "participate in the sufferings of Christ" and we are blessed when we are insulted because of his name.[f]

By God's grace, we will hopefully be given opportunities to show our critics that we are not homophobic, and how truly loved all people are, both by us and our Father God.

---

[1] David Ast et al., *Challenging Homophobia and Heterosexism: A K-12 Curriculum Resource Guide* (Toronto: Toronto District School Board, 2011), 202.
[2] "Just Say Yes: Respect," *Coalition for Positive Sexuality*, 1997, http://www.positive.org/JustSayYes/respect.html.
[3] Robert Garofalo, "The Association Between Health Risk Behaviors and Sexual Orientation Among a School-Based Sample of Adolescents," *Pediatrics* 101, no. 5 (1998): 895–902; Travis Salway Hottes, Olivier Ferlatte, and Dionne Gesink, "Suicide and HIV as Leading Causes of Death among Gay and Bisexual Men: A Comparison of Estimated Mortality and Published Research," *Critical Public Health* 25, no. 5 (March 26, 2014): 513–26, http://www.tandfonline.com/eprint/tUFcScrWDudydMQiapTJ/full; Theo G. M. Sandfort, "Same-Sex Sexual Behavior and Psychiatric Disorders," *Archives of General Psychiatry (Journal of the American Medical Association)* 58, no. 1 (January 2001).
[4] Ontario, Ministry of Education, *The Ontario Curriculum, Grades 9-12: Health and Physical Education* (Toronto: Queen's Printer for Ontario, 2015), http://www.edu.gov.on.ca/eng/curriculum/secondary/health9to12.pdf, 126.

---

[f] 1 Peter 4:13, 14

[5] R. de Graaf, Theo G. M. Sandfort, and M. ten Have, "Suicidality and Sexual Orientation: Differences between Men and Women in a General Population-Based Sample from the Netherlands," *Archives of Sexual Behavior* 35, no. 3 (2006): 253–62.

[6] This has been widely established by many credible sources, e.g., Gary J. Gates, "Gay People Count, So Why Not Count Them Correctly?" *The Washington Post,* April 11, 2011, https://www.washingtonpost.com/opinions/gay-people-count-so-why-not-count-them-correctly/2011/04/07/AFDg9K4C_story.html?utm_term=.472fbc1a9fbd; Sue Ellin Browder, "Kinsey's Secret: The Phony Science of the Sexual Revolution," Crisis Magazine, May 28, 2012, http://www.crisismagazine.com/2012/kinseys-secret-the-phony-science-of-the-sexual-revolution; Jerry Bergman, "Kinsey, Darwin and the Sexual Revolution," Journal of Creation 20, no. 3 (December 2006): 111–17.

[7] "TIMELINE | Same-Sex Rights in Canada," *CBC News*, Last modified May 25, 2015, http://www.cbc.ca/news/canada/timeline-same-sex-rights-in-canada-1.1147516.

[8] Ontario Human Rights Commission, *Policy on Discrimination and Harassment Because of Sexual Orientation* (Toronto: Queen's Printer for Ontario, 2006), http://www.ohrc.on.ca/sites/default/files/attachments/Policy_on_discrimination_and_harassment_because_of_sexual_orientation.pdf.

[9] "TIMELINE | Same-Sex Rights in Canada."

[10] OHRC, "Gender Identity and Gender Expression," accessed January 24, 2017, http://www.ohrc.on.ca/en/code_grounds/gender_identity.

[11] Statistics Canada, "Same-Sex Couples and Sexual Orientation... by the Numbers," Last modified November 9, 2016, http:/www.statcan.gc.ca/eng/dai/smr08/2015/smr08_203_2015.

[12] "Trinity Western Law School Decision Overturned by B.C. Supreme Court," *CBC News*, December 10, 2015, http://www.cbc.ca/news/canada/british-columbia/trinity-western-law-society-bc-supreme-court-1.3359942.

[13] OHRC, *Emerging Human Rights Protections* in the *Policy on Preventing Discrimination and Harassment because of Gender Identity and Gender Expression* (Toronto: Queen's Printer for Ontario, 2014), http://www.ohrc.on.ca/en/policy-preventing-discrimination-because-gender-identity-and-gender-expression/5-emerging-human-rights-protections, 11.

[14] Canada, Parliament, House of Commons, "An Act to Amend the Canadian Human Rights Act and the Criminal Code," Pub. L. No. C-16 (2015), http://www.parl.gc.ca/HousePublications/Publication.aspx?Language=E&Mode=1&DocId=8609176.

[15] Ibid.

[16] Ontario, Attorney General, *Human Rights Code* (Toronto: Queen's Printer for Ontario, 2016), last modified December 5, 2016, 4, http://du0tsrdospf80.cloudfront.net/docs/90h19_e.doc.

[17] OHRC, *Guide to your Rights and Responsibilities under the Human Rights Code,* (Toronto: Queen's Printer for Ontario, 2009), last modified January 15, 2009, 7. http://www.ohrc.on.ca/sites/default/files/guide%20to%20your%20rights%20and%20responsibilities%20under%20the%20human%20rights%20code_1.pdf.

[18] OHRC, "OHRC Remarks to the Ontario Legislative Standing Committee on Social Policy Regarding Bill 13 and Bill 14," May 15, 2012, http://www.ohrc.on.ca/en/ohrc-remarks-ontario-legislative-standing-committee-social-policy-regarding-bill-13-and-bill-14.

[19] Ontario, Ministry of Education, *The Ontario Curriculum, Grades 1-8, Language* (Toronto: Queen's Printer for Ontario, 2006), http://www.edu.gov.on.ca/eng/curriculum/elementary/language18currb.pdf.

[20] Ontario, Ministry of Education, *The Ontario Curriculum, Grades 1-8: The Arts* (Toronto: Queen's Printer for Ontario, 2009), 38, 50, 137, http://www.edu.gov.on.ca/eng/curriculum/elementary/arts18b09curr.pdf.

[21] Ast et al., *Challenging Homophobia and Heterosexism*, 2.

[22] OHRC, "OHRC Remarks to the Ontario Legislative Standing Committee."

[23] Ontario, Ministry of Education, "Creating Safe and Accepting Schools: Information for Parents about the Accepting Schools Act (Bill 13)" (Toronto: Queen's Printer for Ontario, 2012), http://www.edu.gov.on.ca/eng/safeschools/SafeAccepSchools.pdf.

[24] Ontario, Ministry of Education, "Policy/Program Memorandum No. 145: Progressive Discipline and Promoting Positive Student Behaviour," December 5, 2012, http://www.edu.gov.on.ca/extra/eng/ppm/145.pdf.

[25] Ontario, Ministry of Education, *The Ontario Curriculum / Social Studies, Grades 1 to 6; History and Geography, Grades 7 and 8* (Toronto: Queen's Printer for Ontario, 2013), http://www.edu.gov.on.ca/eng/curriculum/elementary/sshg18curr2013.pdf, 202.

[26] Ontario, Ministry of Education, *The Ontario Curriculum / Social Studies, Grades 1 to 6; History and Geography, Grades 7 and 8*, 78.

[27] Ibid.

[28] Ontario, Ministry of Education, Kathleen Wynne in *Realizing the Promise of Diversity: Ontario's Equity and Inclusive Education Strategy* (Toronto: Queen's Printer for Ontario, 2009), 2. http://www.edu.gov.on.ca/eng/policyfunding/equity.pdf.

[29] Caleb Kaltenbach, *Messy Grace* (Colorado Springs: Water Brook Press, 2015).

[30] "Accept," *Dictionary.com*, April 11, 2015, http://dictionary.reference.com/browse/accept?s=t.

[31] Ontario, Ministry of Education, *The Ontario Curriculum, Grades 1-8: Health and Physical Education* (Toronto: Queen's Printer for Ontario, 2015), http://www.edu.gov.on.ca/eng/curriculum/elementary/health1to8.pdf, 232.

Chapter 2

THE CULTURAL SHIFT

"Then Jesus said to his disciples, 'Whoever wants to be my disciple must deny themselves and take up their cross and follow me.'"

Matthew 16:24

It took some nerve to re-introduce the sex education curriculum in Ontario in 2015. Premier Dalton McGuinty first presented an updated curriculum in 2010 and within 54 hasty hours, retracted his decision, shelving it indefinitely. Parents in Ontario had stated loud and clear that they had no intentions of allowing something so radical to be taught to their children in the public school system.

In 2015, Kathleen Wynne brought the shelved curriculum back. In spite of an equal uproar by parents and other citizens, she doesn't appear to be wavering in the least in her decision to stand by the curriculum. What has changed? Is it simply the dogged determination of Premier Wynne? Or even in those few short years, have gradual shifts in cultural thinking led to the general acceptance of the ideology of comprehensive sex education?

The Cultural Shift – Sexual Orientation

The concept that differing sexual orientations are a natural part of the human experience has had a head start over transgenderism in being understood and accepted by the culture.

Just to make sure we are all on the same page, let's look at the definition of sexual orientation according to the Ontario curriculum: "a person's sense of sexual attraction to people of the same sex, the opposite sex, or both sexes."[1] *Gender Diversity.org* further clarifies the culture's position that "our sexual orientation and our gender identity are separate, distinct parts of our overall identity."[2]

There is generally agreed to be a range of sexual orientations that include **homosexual, bisexual,** and **heterosexual.** However, the concept of sexual orientation, like gender identity, seems to be broadening. Recently on a prime-time CBC sitcom, many Canadians were introduced to the idea of **pansexualism** – the concept that a person is equally attracted to and willing to engage in sex with both sexes and genders, for example, attraction to a homosexual male on one occasion or a heterosexual transgendered female on another.[3] Have you heard of **skoliosexual?** These are people who are only attracted to others who do not conform to sexual or gender roles. Confused? Me too.

The Importance of the Truth

There is a range of numbers used to estimate how many people are lesbian, gay, or bisexual. The most widely used figure is 10%, an amount first put forward by the Kinsey Report in 1948.[4] Although this flawed and disturbing study has been disproven time and again,[5] the 10% is still generally accepted as factual. This is problematic and misleading on many levels. See the following quote from KidsHealth, a website that gets more than a million hits a day from people looking for answers about children's health issues:

> Being straight, gay, or bisexual is **not** something that a person can choose or choose to change. In fact, people don't choose their sexual orientation any more than they choose their height or eye color. It is estimated that about 10% of people are gay.[6]

In contrast, a 2014 Statistics Canada (StatCan) survey found that of Canadians aged 17-59, 1.7% consider themselves to be gay or lesbian, and 1.3% consider themselves to be bisexual.[7] Let's do the math: 1.7 + 1.3 = 3. Three percent.

While teaching grade seven a number of years ago, I sat in on a class meeting with a fellow staff member who was dealing with a bullying issue, including the use of the word "gay" among boys in the change room. I still remember her quoting the 10% statistic to drive the point home about how inappropriate this was. Her message was, "Did you know that 10% of people are gay? In this group of thirty kids, that means three of you are gay." The kids began muttering right away.

In a group of thirty kids, using StatCan's 3%, 0.9 students in the room would be gay (or bisexual). *Less than one* student in the room would be gay or bisexual, not three. A more accurate message (if you were to use this questionable strategy) is, "There's a chance that one person in the room may one day identify as gay, lesbian, or bisexual." What a potential difference when people are told a lie – no matter how sincerely the teller believes it – instead of the truth. Numbers matter. True facts matter.

"But I was Born this Way!"

The Lady Gaga hit, "Born This Way," was an anthem in the 2016 Toronto Pride parade, with Canadian Prime Minister Justin Trudeau joining in the song during the pre-parade church service.[8] Here are some of the lyrics.

> It doesn't matter if you love him or capital H-I-M
> Just put your paws up
> 'Cause you were born this way, baby
>
> Don't hide yourself in regret
> Just love yourself and you're set
> Don't be drag, just be a queen
> Whether you're broke or evergreen
>
> No matter gay, straight or bi
> Lesbian, transgendered life
> I'm on the right track, baby
> I was born to survive
>
> I'm beautiful in my way
> 'Cause God makes no mistakes
> I'm on the right track, baby
> I was born this way[9]

Human sexuality is predictable but not absolute. Most people – an overwhelming majority of people – engage in exclusively heterosexual behaviour. However, as we are reminded almost daily: some people are gay.

Lady Gaga's anthem is just one of the pop songs, slogans, and undisputed rhetoric that proclaim: "This is how I was born!" The uncomfortable question is whether that is actually true. So much hinges on this, yet in our society questioning this is almost unforgivable.

Most of us know at least one man, homosexual or not, who has always been more on the feminine side, or a tomboy who didn't really surprise you when she came out. We secretly (or not so secretly) affirm people in their choice to identify as LGBT because we have observed traits that we believe align with that identity. We may even feel smug because we "knew" before the person "came out." In this chapter and the chapters ahead, we will see how important it is that we challenge this mindset!

The Cultural Shift

A couple of years ago, I was having dinner with a group of people I have known for a long time. One of them, a friend I had grown up with, had come out of the closet as homosexual and had married his partner. In the course of conversation, one of the party commented to our friend that she had not been surprised when he came out of the closet, that she "always knew" he was gay.

Since this had not been my experience with this friend, I was surprised on several levels by her remark. Perhaps it was my naiveté or perhaps it was the fact that my friend (like me) had been brought up as a Christian, involved in missions, and even attended Bible college. Being gay hadn't been on my radar for him. The truth is, I was completely unaware of his struggle.

People are not required to assume an identity that labels them by their struggle.

Although I had not yet begun to put much thought into the issue, something made me uncomfortable with the statement that this woman made, that she "always knew" he was gay. Was she trying to tell him that she believed he was born that way and to affirm that his identifying and living as a gay man was inevitable and right? If so, was such affirmation in his best interest? Did it ultimately help him? She obviously believed that it would.

When and how people come to the conclusion that they are attracted to the same sex varies. Many relate this experience from the time they were children. Others may hit puberty before they realize they aren't as interested in the opposite sex as everyone else seems to be. Sometimes a person doesn't experience a same-sex attraction until he or she is an adult.

As tempting as it is to dwell on the question of whether or not someone is born that way, let's resist going further down that path. Suffice it to say that scientists have not discovered a gay gene,[10] nor are prenatal hormone changes a conclusive factor in determining homosexuality.¹¹ I have heard it discussed and agree that being attracted to people of the same sex is, in fact, the way original sin plays out in some people's lives.¹² All of us have our own sin struggle. For some, it is same-sex attraction.

I have come to believe that the answer to the "born that way" question, as much as it matters when talking about the reason for same-sex attraction, *shouldn't* matter with regard to ultimate choices and actions. Why is that? Being inclined toward same-sex attraction does not require a person to act on it any more than we are required to follow other temptations to sin. If we believe homosexual practices are sinful, we have to trust that the temptation to engage in these practices comes with a way out, as God has promised.[a] As well, people are not required to assume an identity that labels them by their sin struggle.

To Be or Not to Be

The cultural shift towards homosexuality in the past 60 years is rooted in the belief that because a person *feels* a certain way, he must *act* that way, and should also *identify* that way. In fact, there are four accepted milestones in assuming an LGB identity:

1. Recognizing that you have same-sex attraction
2. Initiating a same-sex sexual or intimate experience
3. Disclosing your non-heterosexual orientation to others
4. Identifying as LGB¹³

Let's try to poke some holes in this progression.

No/Little Choice. A man who has effeminate build or speech; a little girl who acts or looks like a tomboy; abuse or childhood expe-

---

[a] "No temptation has overtaken you except what is common to mankind. And God is faithful; he will not let you be tempted beyond what you can bear. But when you are tempted, he will also provide a way out so that you can endure it." (1 Corinthians 10:13)

riences which cause sexual or gender confusion; experiencing same-sex attraction at some period of life; a life-long struggle with same-sex attraction; battling a desire to dress or self-express as the opposite gender, and so forth.

Choice. Acting on those impulses and/or ultimately assuming an LGBT identity.

In the next chapter, we will discuss the critical point of identity, and introduce the concept of "lie-dentity" but first let's take a look at how the confusion surrounding gender identity has evolved in our culture.

The Cultural Shift – Gender Identity

In the Ontario curriculum, **gender** is defined as "a term that refers to those characteristics of women and men that are socially constructed."[14] In contrast, **sex** refers to "the category of male or female, based on characteristics that are biologically determined."[15]

Since gender is viewed as a social construct, then one can choose whether to go along with behaviours and expressions that correspond socially to their biological sex. If they choose not to, then they can identify with any number of other possible genders. The curriculum lists six possibilities: male, female, **two-spirited**, **transgender**, **transsexual**, and **intersex**[16] but there appear to be many more possible gender identities. In 2014, Facebook introduced 56 different genders but has since transitioned to giving users a choice of Male/Female/Custom (blank entry field), and identifying a preferred pronoun.

The Gender-Bread Person

A common model called "The Genderbread Person" is cropping up in various Ministry of Education and school board documents. It is being used to clarify the different identities and orientations to the average layperson.[17]

The Genderbread Person tells us that gender identity is "how you, in your head, define your gender, based on how much you align (or don't align) with what you understand to be the options for gender."[18] A man who is sensitive and cries easily might feel like he is aligned to "woman-ness." A competitive woman with strong leadership skills might feel like she relates more with "man-ness." *This is the internal impression of our gender.*

Gender expression is defined as "the ways you present gender, through your actions, dress, and demeanor and how those presentations are interpreted based on gender norms."[19] A buzzed haircut can be seen as an expression of masculinity. Wearing a skirt or makeup can be seen as a feminine expression. *This is the outward expression of our gender.*

In the Genderbread Person, a person is a blank slate with which one can design an identity based on personal preferences and style. Everything is an option – preferred genitalia, roles in relationship or parenting, clothes worn, and gestures and expressions used. Everything can be defined at the discretion of the individual. The new normal is that *there is no normal.*

Gender diversity encourages us to give people space to identify anywhere along a continuum from male to female. This concept is foreign to many of us and in order to come to grips with the cultural pressure, we need to examine whether gender is truly negotiable or not.

If gender is negotiable (a social construct), then when a person feels as though their gender doesn't match their biological sex, the compassionate thing would be to support them in transitioning to their **felt gender**. They might do this *socially*, by presenting themselves differently than is typically expected of their biological sex or *medically*, through surgery.

On the flip side, if gender is not negotiable (prescribed), then the same support could lead a friend into a place of serious physical and psychological harm. We can't overlook the fact that the suicide rates

The Cultural Shift

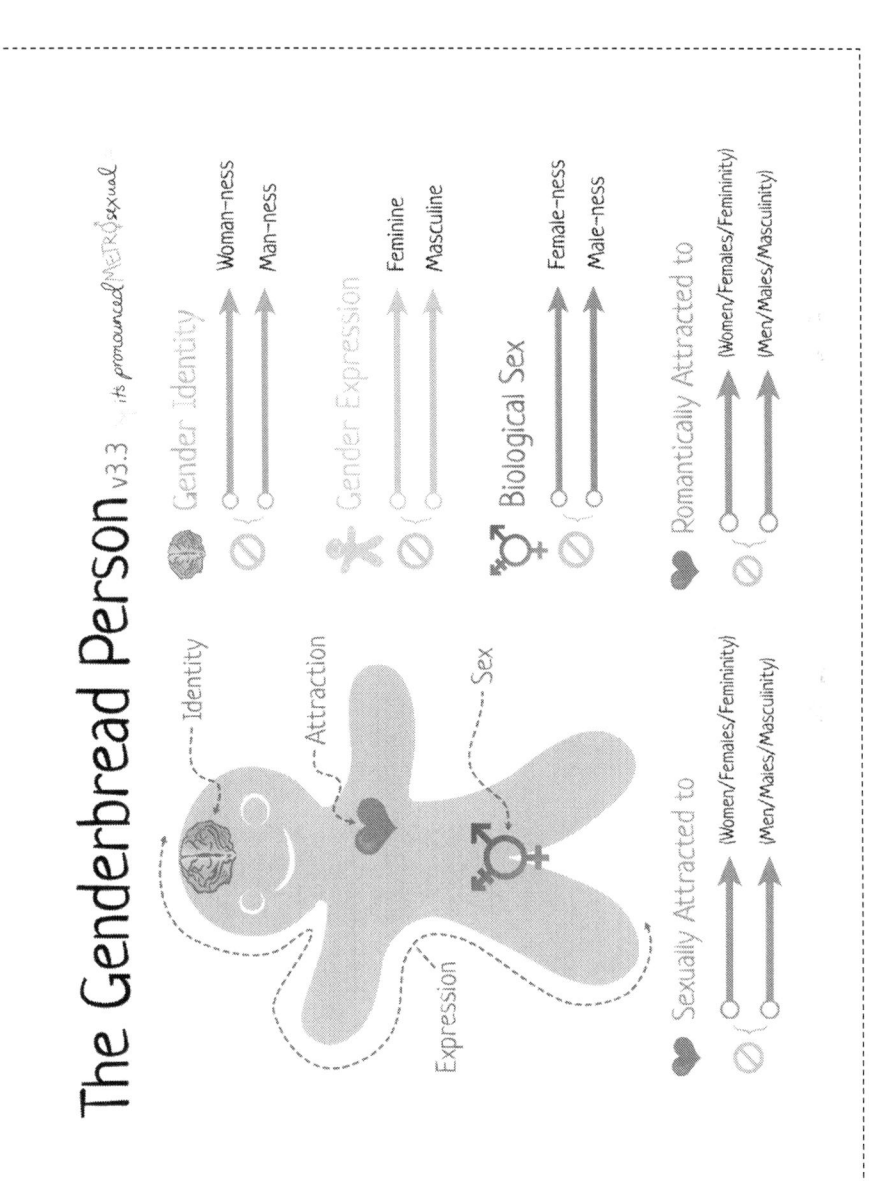

Source: Sam Killerman, "The Genderbread Person v3.3," itspronouncedmetrosexual.com

of those who medically transition to their felt gender are still twenty times higher than the general population.[20]

I believe that although gender does have a social component which determines how each gender is expressed, there are key elements of gender that are prescribed at birth by the simple biology that make our bodies male or female.

Gender Confusion and Dysphoria

What's troubling is that some people begin to struggle to identify with their biological sex as children, some as young as the age of three. The following story is of a child from Edmonton, Alberta.

> The parents said they knew from the beginning that something was different about their child, but last September, the youngster made it clear.
>
> "I just told my mom I felt like a girl," the seven-year-old recalled. That's when her parents say they knew their child wasn't "a boy who liked girl toys – she was a girl who had a penis," said the child's mother ...
>
> "As soon as she could speak, she would articulate that she is a female and would gravitate towards feminine objects," the mother said.
>
> "We just assumed it was a phase at the time. We weren't educated about what it meant to be transgender."[21]

According to the website *tolerance.org*, some children "know their gender identity and birth sexes do not match almost as soon as they begin to talk."[22] Some children view themselves along a spectrum somewhere between male and female, whereas others wish to be the opposite sex entirely. These children are spoken of in different terms such as "gender independent, gender creative, gender expansive and gender diverse."[23]

The child described above has what psychologists previously called gender identity disorder[b] but would now refer to as **gender dysphoria**. Dr. Don Horrocks of the Evangelical Alliance describes gender dysphoria as "an overwhelming psychological belief that [an individual] will feel better, and be more able to accept themselves, if they were of the opposite sex."[24] People who have gender dysphoria are often described as being transgendered.

To activists, gender confusion as a *disorder* feels negative. Descriptions such as *creative* and *expansive* feel positive. However, these words do little to communicate the distress of children who do not want to dress, play, or even urinate like those of their birth sex, or are so disgusted by the sight of their genitals that they wish to get rid of them.[25]

Like people who struggle with same-sex attraction, people who struggle with their gender are in emotional pain. This shouldn't be surprising. They have rejected something which is core to their identity. Canadian psychiatrist Dr. Kenneth Zucker, a world-leading specialist in treating children with gender dysphoria, tells of a young girl who expressed disgust with her body by punching her vagina in anger, and it is not uncommon for children with gender dysphoria to self-harm in this way.[26] This personal rejection, coupled with potential rejection by those around them, can cause incredible emotional anguish.

What Gender Confusion Is Not

The rare conditions known collectively as intersex have been used to prop up the idea that gender is not strictly biological. This

---

[b] The switch from "gender identity disorder" to "gender dysphoria" happened in 2013. "Replacing 'disorder' with 'dysphoria' ... removes the connotation that the patient is 'disordered'... the critical element of gender dysphoria is the presence of clinically significant distress associated with the condition." See "Gender Dysphoria," in *Diagnostic and Statistical Manual of Mental Disorders (DSM-5)*, American Psychiatric Association (2013).

connection, rather, has been constructed largely from convenience rather than the hard evidence and life experiences of those affected by one of these conditions.

What is intersex? It can be a variety of conditions ranging from almost undetectable (the affected individual remains unaware throughout life that they have one of these conditions) to substantial (often requiring surgery). Intersex conditions can affect external genitals, internal reproductive organs, sex chromosomes, or sex-related hormones.[27] Those requiring surgery often have abnormally developed sex organs.

Intersex conditions are, simply put, a mistake in the genetic code. Like all genetic conditions, from cystic fibrosis to cleft lip, it is a genetic anomaly that exists only because of the Fall. Intersex is not, as some people or cultures suggest, a third gender but rather a varying combination of the two sexes in one body. And yet, in spite of the somewhat unusual nature of their sex organs, these individuals are no more likely to identify as transgendered than the rest of the population.[28] Even though some intersex individuals are actually born with sexual organs of both sexes, most of them easily identify with their genetic sex – now identifiable through DNA testing. There is generally no sense of gender dysphoria. For many who are intersex, their condition is a very small part of their lives and most reject being lumped in by default with the LGBT community.

Why Are Children Confused About Their Gender?

There are children like the child from Edmonton you read about earlier, who are confused about their gender. We can't deny this. The crucial question is how we help these children figure out and come to terms with who they are. The reality is that science can't yet explain why some children reject their biological gender. There are a number of theories on the table.

Biological Reasons

Dr. Carys Massarella, a medical doctor who is also a male-to-female transgender, sees transgenderism as natural, "not an illness or something needing to be fixed but rather part of the rich diversity of human experience."[29] Dr. Massarella suggests that children who are confused about their gender should be given the space they need to express themselves and be nourished in a supportive environment.[30] (S)he argues that when a person experiences gender dysphoria, there is "no diagnosis needed" because there is "no measurable biological effect in a negative way."[31] As a specialist in this field, the process (s)he follows is to "allow transgender people to claim their identity, and then provide safe and medically appropriate access to cross gender hormone therapy and surgery, plus support through transition."[32] In essence, Dr. Massarella is stating that gender dysphoria is a normal experience that is not a diagnosable illness or disorder, yet (s)he encourages access to medical treatment to correct it. Charlotte, who has a background in healthcare, was flabbergasted by this reasoning. Even I know that in order to receive treatment, I must first be diagnosed with something. Without a diagnosis, it's hard to understand how a treatment can be prescribed, and hormone therapy and surgery are certainly a form of treatment!

Further looking into biological causes, I found that some studies suggest physical differences between the brains of transgendered and other men.[33] There is also research that refutes that.[34] For example, there is a tiny section of the brain called the BSTc. A group of scientists reported that in transgendered men (transfemale) this section is more similar in size to women than to other men, which suggests a potential genetic cause for transgenderism.[35] Ironically, one of the same scientists published an article seven years later reporting that significant size changes do not occur until adulthood.[36] This suggests that perhaps **transfemale** men, who of course do not develop a positive male gender identity, experience a decrease in size of the BSTc as a result of indulging feminine thought patterns.[37]

This idea is supported by research which has confirmed that a specific area of the brain called the hippocampus will physically grow if "exercised" (for example by repeated use of complex information) and then later shrink if the need for that information is no longer required.[c][38] If the hippocampus can be enlarged with use then perhaps the size of the BSTc may also be affected by how the area is used by the individual, and not by genetics.

Finally, there are theories that insufficient testosterone or a genetic mutation affects a preborn boy's ability to absorb testosterone in the womb which may result in a transgendered child.[39] But this same mutation occurs in 35-51% of other men who do not identify as transgendered.[40] There is obviously more at play.

Psychological Reasons

There are experts who have spent years working with transgendered individuals and we can learn a lot from their experience. Dr. Paul McHugh is one such expert, spending forty years at John Hopkins Medical School, twenty-six as Psychiatrist in Chief at John Hopkins Hospital. In his experience, gender dysphoria can be compared to other body disorders such as anorexia nervosa. He compares the idea of suggesting sex-change surgery for a transgendered patient to suggesting liposuction for an anorexic patient. In short, it creates a new set of serious issues and does nothing to treat the original problem. He recommends treatment that resolves the distorted *thinking* the person has about their body rather than treating them as though the issue is truly with the *body* itself.[41]

Dr. Susan Bradley, another leading expert, has treated over 400 children with gender dysphoria in Toronto. Dr. Bradley has often seen gender dysphoria paired with other conditions such as autism

---

[c] For a fascinating read on how this works, google "The Knowledge" and "London Taxi Drivers.", e.g., http://voices.nationalgeographic.com / 2013/05/29/the-bigger-brains-of-london-taxi-drivers/.

or obsessive-compulsive disorder, something that has also been observed by the World Professional Association for Transgender Health.[42] Like Dr. McHugh, Dr. Bradley observed that gender dysphoria usually looks and behaves in a way that is similar to behavioural issues and eating disorders. Bradley has also treated children for other identity issues including wanting to be an animal or a number, something that is readily recognized as a false mindset. She says, "We've done a lot of studies, we've looked at these kids up and down and can find no evidence this is an inherent issue."[43]

Reasons of Abuse or Trauma

Walt Heyer has another perspective. As a young boy, he was secretly dressed as a girl by his grandmother and came to believe he was a girl in a boy's body – that his true identity was female. He underwent sex reassignment surgery to become a woman and again years later, to return to living as a man.[44]

Heyer believes "children cannot be born as one gender and identify as another by accident."[45] He now performs outreach to individuals experiencing gender dysphoria. Some individuals he has worked with have pointed to an event or series of events as the source of their struggle: abuse (sexual, physical or other), neglect, trauma, or even an overbearing parent. Heyer says of his experience, "My grandmother kept cross-dressing me and loving on me as a girl and not as the boy God made,"[46] which had a significant negative effect on his gender development.

The Final Analysis

I have come to the conclusion that no matter what your point of view, if you look hard enough you will find a scientific study or an expert opinion that will support your preconceptions. This is true for both Christian and secular sides of the debate. When addressing conflicting or controversial issues, it is important for Christians to be informed but also to remember that our ultimate source of truth comes from God's Word.

Bill 77

Sexual orientation was declassified as a psychiatric condition in 1973 and therapy to "cure" homosexuality is not only controversial but is generally agreed to be infective. Gender identity disorder, now declassified to gender dysphoria, may also soon be removed as a psychiatric condition by the Psychiatric Association.

What can be done to help children with gender dysphoria or who are confused about their sexuality? Start by knowing that treatment to address any psychological root issues (such as that previously offered by practitioners such as Drs. Zucker and Bradley) is in fact now *illegal* in Ontario, and is heading that way in other provinces and states. Ontario's Bill 77, *The Affirming Sexual Orientation and Gender Identity Act 2015,* has declared that if a child feels that his or her true gender is opposite to their physical gender, it is an offence for a medical or psychological practitioner to provide treatment that will help align that person's felt gender to their physical gender, *even if this is what he or she wants.*[47]

Take for example a Christian therapist who provides a wide variety of counseling services but will also counsel Christians who struggle with same-sex attraction or gender dysphoria. This therapist would no longer be able to continue in a professional, registered capacity if he or she did anything less but affirm the LGBT identity. This bill is not only a shame for capable, caring medical professionals but also for sincere individuals who are seeking help.

What's absurd about Bill 77 is that both sides of the issue agree that most children who experience gender dysphoria will not end up being transgendered! Most children who have some sort of gender confusion will come to identify with their biological gender as they grow up.[48, 49] Even Dr. Massarella agrees with this![50]

To me, this makes a loud argument *against* encouraging or giving space to the confusion. If our desire is to raise healthy children without emotional baggage from their childhood – or worse, surgical or hormonal bodily change that they may later regret – then shouldn't we coach and support children to come to terms with their biological gender? Or at least, not actively encourage them otherwise?

The parents of "John," a child who was diagnosed with gender dysphoria would certainly think so. "John" was treated by Dr. Zucker of the former Child and Adolescent Gender Identity Clinic in Toronto,[51] a clinic that has since been shut down due to accusations that it was not progressive enough.[52] "John" was a success story, many are.[53] His gender dysphoria diminished and eventually disappeared.

The Association for Reformed Political Action is a grassroots Canadian organization whose goal is, in part, to bring a biblical perspective to civil authorities.[54] It affirms that "to leave the dysphoria untreated is to leave struggling individuals without help, and to ignore experienced researchers in this field."[55] Is this something we can do in good conscience? It's my belief that Bill 77 represents a true atrocity for the people of Ontario.

As Christians, we have an amazing opportunity. The world around us is grappling with confusion, seeking answers about its significance and identity through self-awareness and permissiveness. We already know the source of these answers! God has clearly told us who we really are. As our wise Creator, he is the one most qualified to speak to each person's purpose and identity.

By becoming aware of what God has to say about our identity, including the gender he gave us at our conception, we learn about our true identity in the chaos of a culture that is truly spinning out of control. Let's take a close look at this next.

[1] Ontario, Ministry of Education, *The Ontario Curriculum, Grades 1-8: Health and Physical Education* (Toronto: Queen's Printer for Ontario, 2015), 232, http://www.edu.gov.on.ca/eng/curriculum/elementary/health1to8.pdf.

[2] "Terminology," *Gender Diversity*, 2016, http://www.genderdiversity.org/resources/terminology/.

[3] *Schitt's Creek*, no. 1-10, "Honeymoon," TV show, first broadcast Match 10, 2015 by the CBC, Directed by Jerry Ciccoritti and written by Daniel Levy.

[4] Alfred Kinsey, Wardell Pomeroy and Clyde Martin, *Sexual Behavior in the Human Male*, (Philadelphia: W. B. Saunders, 1948).

[5] Browder, "Kinsey's Secret: The Phony Science of the Sexual Revolution"; Bergman, "Kinsey, Darwin and the Sexual Revolution -."

[6] "Sexual Orientation," *KidsHealth*, 2017, http://kidshealth.org/en/parents/sexual-orientation.html.

[7] Statistics Canada, "Canadian Community Health Survey - Annual Component (CCHS)," June 24, 2016, http://www23.statcan.gc.ca/imdb/p2SV.pl?Function=getSurvey&SDDS=3226.

[8] The Canadian Press, "Justin Trudeau at Pride Toronto: 'We Can't Let Hate Go By'," *Macleans*, July 3, 2016, http://www.macleans.ca/news/canada/justin-trudeau-at-pride-toronto-we-cant-let-hate-go-by/.

[9] Lady Gaga, "Born This Way," Written by *Stefani Germanotta*, Jeppe Laursen, Fernando Garibay, Paul Blair, Sony/ATV Music Publishing LLC, Warner/Chappell Music, Inc., Universal Music Publishing Group, 2011, accessed on *Metro Lyrics*, http://www.metrolyrics.com/born-this-way-lyrics-lady-gaga.html

[10] Ed Yong, "No, Scientists Have Not Found the Gay Gene," *The Atlantic*, Octover10. 2015, https://www.theatlantic.com/science/archive/2015/10/no-scientists-have-not-found-the-gay-gene/410059/.

[11] Melissa Hines, "Prenatal Endocrine Influences on Sexual Orientation and On Sexually Differentiated Childhood Behavior," Frontiers in Neuroendocrinology, 32, no. 2 (2011):170-182, https://www.ncbi.nlm.nih.gov/pmc/articles/PMC3296090/.

[12] Jim Daly, "Navigating Sexual Sin to Find Your Identity in Christ (Part 2 of 2), radio broadcast, first broadcast, January 11, 2017, by Focus on the Family, http://www.focusonthefamily.com/media/daily-broadcast/navigating-sexual-sin-to-find-your-identity-in-christ-pt2.

[13] Heather Corliss et al., "Age of Minority Sexual Orientation Development and Risk of Childhood Maltreatment and Suicide Attempts in Women," *The American Journal of Orthopsychiatry*, 79, no. 4 (2009): 511–521, http://pubmedcentralcanada.ca/pmcc/articles/PMC3375131/

[14] Ontario, Ministry of Education, *The Ontario Curriculum, Grades 1-8: Health and Physical Education*, 231.

[15] Ibid.

[16] Ibid., 216.

[17] Sam Killerman, "The Genderbread Person v3," *It's Pronounced METROsexual*, 2015, http://itspronouncedmetrosexual.com/2015/03/the-genderbread-person-v3/.

[18] Ibid.

[19] Ibid.
[20] Cecilia Dhejne et al., "Long-Term Follow-Up of Transsexual Persons Undergoing Sex Reassignment Surgery: Cohort Study in Sweden," ed. James Scott, *PLoS ONE*, 6, no. 2, e16885 (February 22, 2011), http://journals.plos.org/plosone/article?id=10.1371/journal.pone.0016885.
[21] "Edmonton Catholic School Bans Transgender Child, 7, from Girls' Washroom," *CBC News, Edmonton*, May 14, 2015, http://www.cbc.ca/news/canada/edmonton/edmonton-catholic-school-bans-transgender-child-7-from-girls-washroom-1.3073737.
[22] Carrie Kilman, "The Gender Spectrum," *Teaching Tolerance: A Project of the Southern Poverty Law Center*, Summer 2013, http://www.tolerance.org/gender-spectrum.
[23] Ibid.
[24] Mark Woods, "Transgender and Christian: How Caitlyn Jenner Challenges the Church," *Christian Today*, June 3, 2015, http://www.christiantoday.com/article/transgender.and.christian.how.caitlyn.jenner.challenges.the.church/55334.htm.
[25] Joseph Goldberg, "Gender Dysphoria: What It Is and How It's Treated," *WebMD*, September 9, 2016, http://www.webmd.com/mental-health/gender-dysphoria#1.
[26] "Barbara Kay: Bill 77, the Affirming Sexual Orientation and Gender Identity Act, Is a Dangerous Overreach," *National Post*, June 2, 2015, http://news.nationalpost.com/full-comment/barbara-kay-bill-77-the-affirming-sexual-orientation-and-gender-identity-act-is-a-dangerous-overreach.
[27] Margaret Schneider et al., "Answers to Your Questions About Individuals With Intersex Conditions" (American Psychological Association, 2006), https://www.apa.org/topics/lgbt/intersex.pdf.
[28] "Suggestions for Writing about Intersex," *Intersex Society of North America*, 2008, http://www.isna.org/node/977.
[29] Helen Victoros, Kelly Hayes, and Izida Zorde, "Creating Safe and Inclusive Schools for Gender Independent Children: Interview with Dr. Carys Massarella," *ETFO Voice*, Summer 2012, http://etfovoice.ca/node/50.
[30] Ibid.
[31] Monika Kowalska, "Interview with Carys Massarella," *Heroines of My Life*, April 13, 2014, http://theheroines.blogspot.ca/2014/04/interview-with-carys-massarella.html.
[32] Ibid.
[33] Jessica Hamzelou, "Transsexual Differences Caught on Brain Scan," *New Scientist*, January 26, 2011, https://www.newscientist.com/article/dn20032-transsexual-differences-caught-on-brain-scan.
[34] Ivanka Savic and Stefan Arver, "Sex Dimorphism of the Brain in Male-to-Female Transsexuals," *Oxford Journals*, 2015, http://cercor.oxfordjournals.org/content/early/2011/04/05/cercor.bhr032.full.
[35] Jiang-Ning Zhou, Michel Hofman, Louis Gooren and Dick Swaab, "A Sex Difference in the Human Brain and Its Relation to Transsexuality," *Nature* 378 (November 1995): 68–70, http://www.nature.com/nature/journal/v378/n6552/abs/378068a0.html.
[36] Wilson Chung, Geert De Vries, and Dick Swaab, "Sexual Differentiation of the Bed Nucleus of the Stria Terminalis in Humans May Extend into Adulthood," *The Journal of Neurosci-*

ence 22, no. 3 (February 2002): 1027–33, https://www.researchgate.net/publication/11534454_Sexual_differentiation_of_the_bed_nucleus_of_the_stria_terminalis_in_humans_may_extend_into_adulthood.

[37] Helen Phillips and Philip Cohen, "Boy meets girl," *New Scientist* 170, no 2290 (May 12, 2001): 28.

[38] Dan Stone, "The Bigger Brains of London Taxi Drivers," *National Geographic Magazine*, May 29, 2013, http://voices.nationalgeographic.com/2013/05/29/the-bigger-brains-of-london-taxi-drivers/.

[39] Lauren Hare et al., "Androgen Receptor Repeat Length Polymorphism Associated with Male-to-Female Transsexualism," *Biological Psychiatry* 65, no. 1 (January 1, 2009): 93–96, http://pubmedcentralcanada.ca/pmcc/articles/PMC3402034/.

[40] Ibid.

[41] Paul McHugh, "Transgenderism: A Pathogenic Meme," *The Witherspoon Institute: Public Discourse*, 2015, http://www.thepublicdiscourse.com/2015/06/15145/.

[42] E. Coleman et al., "Standards of Care for the Health of Transsexual, Transgender, and Gender-Nonconforming People, Version 7," *International Journal of Transgenderism* 13, no. 4 (2012): 165–232, https://s3.amazonaws.com/amo_hub_content/Association140/files/Standards%20of%20Care%20V7%20-%202011%20WPATH%20(2)(1).pdf.

[43] Jessica Smith, "Prominent Psychiatrist Speaks Out against Conversion Therapy Legislation," *Metro Toronto*, March 30, 2015, http://www.metronews.ca/news/toronto/2015/03/30/prominent-psychiatrist-speaks-out-against-conversion-therapy-legislation.html.

[44] Walt Heyer, "I Was a Transgender Woman" *The Witherspoon Institute: Public Discourse*, April 1, 2015, http://www.thepublicdiscourse.com/2015/04/14688/.

[45] Lisa Bourne, *"Parents say they're now calling four-year-old son a girl," LifeSiteNews*, July 7, 2015, https://www.lifesitenews.com/news/parents-say-their-now-calling-four-year-old-son-a-girl

[46] Ibid.

[47] Cheri DiNovo, "Bill 77, Affirming Sexual Orientation and Gender Identity Act, 2015," Pub. L. No. 77, 11.2, accessed January 25, 2017, http://www.ontla.on.ca/web/bills/bills_detail.do?locale=en&BillID=3197.

[48] Margaret Wente, "Transgender Kids: Have We Gone Too Far?," *The Globe and Mail*, February 15, 2014, http://www.theglobeandmail.com/opinion/transgender-kids-have-we-gone-too-far/article16897043/.

[49] William Byne et al., "Report of the APA Task Force on Treatment of Gender Identity Disorder." American Journal of Psychiatry 169, no. 4 (2012): data supplement 1-35, https://www.psychiatry.org/File%20Library/Psychiatrists/Directories/Library-and-Archive/resource_documents/rd2012_GID.pdf

[50] Victoros, Hayes, and Zorde, "Creating Safe and Inclusive Schools."

[51] Hanna Rosin, "A Boy's Life," *The Atlantic*, November 2008, https://www.theatlantic.com/magazine/archive/2008/11/a-boys-life/307059/.

[52] Sheryl Ubelacker, "Group Protests Closure of Youth Gender Identity Clinic at CAMH, Director's Removal," *Global News*, January 23, 2016,

http://globalnews.ca/news/2473568/group-protests-closure-of-youth-gender-identity-clinic-at-camh-directors-removal/.
[53] Kelley D. Drummond et al., "A Follow-up Study of Girls with Gender Identity Disorder," *Developmental Psychology* 44, no. 1 (January 2008): 34–45, https://www.researchgate.net/publication/5657572_A_Follow-up _Study _of_Girls _With _Gender_Identity_Disorder.

Chapter 3

OUR TRUE IDENTITY
IN THE CHAOS OF SEXUALITY

"I have been crucified with Christ and I no longer live, but Christ lives in me. The life I now live in the body, I live by faith in the Son of God, who loved me and gave himself for me."

Galatians 2:20

The terms "identity" and "identify" have come up a few times so far and understanding them will give us a true appreciation of the stakes in this cultural battle. From a Biblical perspective, how we identify can mean the difference between spiritual life and spiritual death. Key choices we make impact our identity in far-reaching ways.

Each of us has an identity but how often do we think about it?

Merriam-Webster defines "identity" in part as "the qualities, beliefs, etc., that make a person or group different from others."[1] Our race, culture, and religion are often key parts of our identity. This is because we tend to identify with people who share similar values and with whom we are most familiar.

Our identity, while largely influenced by our genetic make-up or culture, is also formed by decisions we make. As we mature and experience life for ourselves, the things we identify with begin to change and evolve. Some people may come to identify with higher education or income. Still others, fitness, the arts, a career, parenting, work or activism.

How a person's identity develops is influenced by many factors. A happy, love-filled childhood leads to a different sort of identity than do memories of abuse. And consider the difference to an individual's sense of self when his or her talents are nurtured and affirmed, as opposed to an environment of addictions and criticisms that stunt creativity. Also consider that religious, cultural, community, media, and positive and negative family interactions can have significant influence as young identities bud and grow.

Identity

Identification, at its most rudimentary level, is shown on a wallet-sized, plastic card. I'm looking at my driver's licence. It tells others my name, where I live, my height, sex, and date of birth. It has my picture on it, some identifying numbers that are associated with me, and my rights and restrictions as a driver. There's more that could have been included, but these are the pieces that the government has chosen to identify that I am who I say I am. Changing any of the information on the card cannot be done easily nor should the decision to do so be taken lightly.

Perhaps there are some people who go their whole lives without revealing much more than what their driver's licence could tell but most people have a greater story to share. Our story shapes our identity.

For example, my parents and my husband's both immigrated to Canada from the Netherlands. We have the height, hair colour, and share a last name that easily identifies us as having Dutch descent. I can dye my hair or change my name but nothing can change my Dutch ancestry.

My passport, birth certificate, and life experience tell me I am Canadian. If I am dissatisfied with that identity, with considerable difficulty I can change it by applying to become a citizen of, and usually moving to a different country. However, even if I did so, my Canadian heritage would always form part of who I am.

What I follow or join on social media is a good indication of what parts of my identity I most value, and this makes sense. People who share an identity can relate to one another more easily.

When you introduce yourself, what parts of your identity do you include? It depends on the context, doesn't it? Do you tell others you are a nurse, garbage collector, hairdresser, or project manager? How about a runner, crafter, painter, collector, or gardener? A mother, father, granddaughter, sister, brother, cousin, or son? Pro-life, cancer survivor, activist, tree-hugger, fan, follower? How about politics? Are you progressive, conservative, or liberal? Who are you?

Are you a Christian?

Our Changing Identity

As we age and move through the stages of life, our identity is bound to shift. Becoming engaged and getting married activates a major change to our identity. We are choosing to identify with another person in the most intimate and all-encompassing ways. When we get married, we form something new: a family that didn't exist before. Often, the woman takes the man's name, and although some may argue with me, I believe that helps to brand the family as a new unit that is intended to be permanent. If they have children, their identity is significantly impacted as they add the labels of mother or father. Their children, in turn, inherit the unique identity of the family they are born or adopted into.

My friend Kim relates how when she disciplines her children, she draws them into the family identity as something that should inform their decisions. She will say, "We are the Hansons. Others might make that choice. We don't because we have chosen to follow God." It's a powerful way to remind children that they are part of something bigger – a family with a shared identity – and that their actions reflect not just on them as individuals but on all others who bear that identity as well.

> **When we choose to identify as Christians, our identity with Christ must come first. We can no longer identify with sin.**

What about when a family breaks down? Reversing the identification process through divorce has immense cost. From personal experience, I can say that divorce is excruciating, exhausting, and overwhelming. If that's not enough, it is messy, time-consuming, and expensive – and that's just for the adults. The impact on the children cannot be overstated.

Divorce serves as a very real example of the cost of changing our identity. Not all identities are as deeply held and foundational as that of marriage and family but when we consider the impact the dissolution of a marriage has to the people involved, it gives us a better idea of the impact of a change to our identity. It can have a generally positive impact (as in getting married) or a negative impact (as in getting divorced) but there is a cost. When we add to or change our identity, there is almost always a divorce from another part of our identity.

The more deeply we associate with a piece of our identity, the harder it is to change it. A change to how we identify takes commitment and effort, and usually comes at a personal cost. Therefore, as a general rule what we put forward as our identity demonstrates our commitment to that element.

Our Identity in Christ

When we choose to identify with Christ, that identity comes first. It should be what we associate with above all else, and it should also inform whether or not we are able to adopt or retain another element in our identity. Most certainly, we can no longer identify with sin.

The Bible teaches that when we accept salvation in Christ we become a new creation. We receive a new identity. The old is gone, the new is come.[a] The old is crucified in Christ. Dead.[b] Gone. Obliterated. We are adopted into God's family as heirs, children of God.[c] There is no ambiguity.

In becoming a new creation, God remakes us, but we must choose to walk in that truth. We need to recognize that although we have been freed from the grip and power of sin, we are going to wrestle with some of the same temptations we did before coming to Christ.

> You were taught, with regard to your former way of life, to put off your old self, which is being corrupted by its deceitful desires; to be made new in the attitude of your minds; and to put on the new self, created to be like God in true righteousness and holiness.
>
> Therefore each of you must put off falsehood and speak truthfully to your neighbor, for we are all members of one body. 'In your anger do not sin': Do not let the sun go down while you are still angry, and do not give the devil a foothold. Anyone who has been stealing must steal no longer, but must work, doing something

---

[a] 2 Corinthians 5:17
[b] Galatians 2:20
[c] Romans 8:17

useful with their own hands, that they may have something to share with those in need.^d

Is there such a thing as a Christian liar? It is certainly possible to struggle in the area of telling the truth but God's Word says that we must "put off falsehood." With the help of the Holy Spirit, we can learn to be honest and to glorify God through a commitment to the truth. As God is truth, so we who bear his name also strive to be known for honesty and integrity. We cannot allow ourselves to be a liar by identity.

Is there such a thing as a Christian murderer? It's true that some Christians have committed murder in the past. Through God's grace there is forgiveness for that, just as there is forgiveness for other sin. However, a believer in Christ rejects the identity as a murderer and does not go on to murder again (or even hate anyone)[e].

This is not to say that Christians don't sin. Of course we do ... I certainly know that I do! The point is that we move forward in grace, not in sin. When we do sin, we repent and ask God to help us in putting off the sin that ensnares us.[f] Allowing ourselves to continue to identify with sin is "giving the devil a foothold" in our lives. What will he do with that? For starters, he will use it to make us ineffective in sharing our faith, crushed by the weight of the sin we continue to bear.

Identity and Sexuality

Please bear in mind the way we are using the terms gay and lesbian in this book – it is as an *identity*, not an *attraction*. There is no doubt in my mind that there are committed Christians who struggle with

---

[d] Ephesians 4:22-28
[e] 1 John 3:15
[f] Hebrews 12:1

same-sex attraction or have a homosexual background.[2] We started this section by stating that when we choose to identify with Christ, we can no longer identify with sin. It follows that since the Bible clearly labels homosexual acts as sinful, a Christian cannot or should not identify with that sin.

> Or do you not know that wrongdoers will not inherit the kingdom of God? Do not be deceived: Neither the sexually immoral nor idolaters nor adulterers nor men who have sex with men nor thieves nor the greedy nor drunkards nor slanderers nor swindlers will inherit the kingdom of God. *And that is what some of you were.* But you were washed, you were sanctified, you were justified in the name of the Lord Jesus Christ and by the Spirit of our God.[g]

The apostle Paul is saying, "Yes! We all have a history of identifying with sin. Lots of sin and all different types of sin." The chapter goes on to state that a person cannot be united with Christ spiritually and united with a prostitute physically. "Do you not know that your bodies are temples of the Holy Spirit, who is in you, whom you have received from God? You are not your own; you were bought at a price. Therefore honor God with your bodies."[h] It doesn't get much clearer than that.

The fact is that some people are inclined toward same-sex attraction. Why this happens, whether through prenatal development as some people suggest or early life experiences or for no apparent reason other than the "thumbprint of original sin on your life,"[3] doesn't matter for the purposes of this discussion. The critical question is whether or not having this experience means you are gay.

I say it doesn't.

As a Christian, devoted to Christ and committed to following him, you can acknowledge that you experience same-sex attraction.

---

[g] 1 Corinthians 6:9-11, emphasis mine
[h] 1 Corinthians 6:19-20

What you cannot do is give yourself over to the *identity* of being gay or lesbian and engage in the *practices* that go along with that identity. Don't let your struggle become your identity.

Don't Let Your Struggle Become Your Identity

While discussing the topics of this book with a friend, she confided to me that she experienced same-sex attraction as an older teen. She gave me permission to share her story. Raised in a Christian home, she knew Jesus as her Saviour. She also knew that God made men and women to be married and in sexual relationship with one another, and that he prohibits homosexual behaviour. Because of her faith, she refused to allow her attraction to this girl to dominate her thoughts and as time went on, the crush went away.

My friend acknowledges that knowing God's truth kept her from acting on her impulses. Had she done so, she may have lost out on the husband and children she now enjoys, and gained regret and shame. When some may have thought, "I must be a lesbian," she knew she was a child of God capable of overcoming sin. She refused to accept the lie that because she was sexually drawn to another girl, then she must be a lesbian.

The concept of sexual orientation isn't defined as easily as the culture would make it to be. The Ontario Health and Physical Education curriculum says sexual orientation is "a person's sense of sexual attraction to people of the same sex, the opposite sex, or both sexes."[4] What about the friend I referred to above? Should she identify as a bisexual woman because she had a sexual attraction to a girl? Absolutely not! She knows she is a fully heterosexual woman who at one point had a **same-sex attraction** experience.

What about a man who admits to near exclusive attraction to other men but is happily married and monogamous with a woman? What is his orientation? If we talked to this man he might admit that his **sexual orientation** is homosexual but he has chosen a heterosexual lifestyle.[i] He may feel he is oriented towards homosexuality but he has chosen to identify with and practice heterosexuality.

You may have noticed that I am not using the term same-sex attraction interchangeably with other terms such as sexual orientation, or words associated with **sexual identification** like gay, lesbian, or bisexual. Rather, I am using each of these terms in purposefully distinct ways. The terms same-sex attraction, sexual orientation, and sexual identification represent very different mindsets with regards to sexuality.

There is a difference between *identifying* as LGB and *experiencing* same-sex attraction at some point in your life. Likewise, there is a difference between *identifying* as LGB, and *feeling* sexually oriented towards the same sex and having no desire for the opposite sex. Homosexual, gay, or lesbian is how some people describe themselves – it is how they identify. To others, having a same-sex attraction, or even being sexually oriented towards the same sex, is just a part of their life experience, *not a part of their identity.*

Lie-dentity vs. Identity

I've referred to the term "lie-dentity" in passing, and now it's time to tell you what I mean by it.

God essentially gave Charlotte and I this term[j] as we were having one of the hundreds of phone calls we had while writing this book. Using speech-to-text on her phone, Charlotte was transcribing the video testimony of a gay man who had come to Christ.

> I thought that being gay was absolutely who I was. From the core of my being, I believed that's who I was. And then after my conversion, my identity just completely changed and my identity was in Christ.[5]

---

[i] For real-life stories like this, visit http://www.livingout.org.
[j] A Google search shows that this term has been used by others (e.g., Pete Briscoe) in the same sense: any identity that is not from God is a lie-dentity.

Somehow in the process, words blended together as "liedentity." It was an epiphany because that's what we've come to understand about the LGBT identity or any identity that contradicts the truth of God's Word to be: a lie.

In chapter two, we explored the false belief that everyone who experiences same-sex attraction will, or should, end up identifying as gay, lesbian or bisexual, or one of the myriad of other sexual orientations. We want to challenge this line of thinking. We hold the position that when a person is sometimes attracted to the same sex (same-sex attraction) or has no sexual desire for the opposite sex (sexual orientation), this *does not* mean that they must be gay, lesbian or bisexual (sexual identification). We feel that when someone *does* choose to identify in this way, they have accepted a lie-dentity.

This lie-dentity is in conflict with an identity in Christ. It is just as the young man stated in his testimony above, "After my conversion, my identity just completely changed and my identity was in Christ."[6]

The Loving Response to Same-Sex Attraction

It would be a mistake to assume that those facing same-sex attraction are making a choice to do so. As mentioned previously, many people who identify as gay and lesbian often don't remember experiencing anything but same-sex attraction. Research has consistently shown that people who experience same-sex attraction deal with a tremendous amount of guilt and self-shaming and have difficulties coming to terms with their sexuality.[7]

Individuals from Christian and other faith backgrounds that oppose homosexuality on moral or religious grounds often have a harder time accepting that their sexual orientation may be homosexual.[8] They've heard the stories about what happened to the immoral people of Sodom and Gomorrah. They have been told that homosexuals "have no inheritance in the kingdom of God."[k] Sadly, research suggests that children from denominations that are overly condemning of homosexuality have higher rates of depression than those from gay-affirming denominations.[9] It is obvious from this discussion that I am not suggesting we affirm LGBT identities, but it is certainly worthwhile to take stock of our approach to our brothers and sisters in Christ who experience same-sex attraction. Likewise, we have to consider the children in our congregations who may be confused about their sexuality. We haven't been getting this right and it's time to make a change.

I firmly believe that a person's sexual identification (and subsequent sexual practice) is at the core. I will never forget the conversation I had with a friend who came out as a lesbian years ago. She deeply desired a relationship with God, and having grown up in a family of faith, was very spiritual in nature. Her conclusion to her struggle was that she could never please God because he had created her unfit for his love. The despair and grief in that conversation haunts me to this day.

I knew then what I know now but didn't know how to express it. The truth is, it's not sexual desire that determines whether sin comes into play but the decision to act or not act on the desire.

As sexual beings, we all have to exercise restraint with our sexual impulses. As a married heterosexual woman, I have to take care not to let my thoughts dwell on another man and to keep my actions in line with God's Word to avoid the snares of adultery. In our highly sexualized culture, Christian men and women have to work extra hard to keep their thoughts and hearts pure.

So what about Christians who experience same-sex attraction? Is it possible for them to keep their hearts pure?

Let me draw a comparison for you. Let's say *Man A* is a happily married, heterosexual Christian. Sometimes he allows his gaze to

---

[k] 1 Corinthians 6:9-10

linger too long on women other than his wife but he has never made any attempts to seek the attention of another woman. He does admit however that he has fantasized about it. He also has another secret: he regularly views pornography and despite many attempts to stop, feels powerless against his obsession. He has prayed over and over for forgiveness but always seems to fall back into this sin.

Say hello to *Man B*. He had a number of homosexual relationships before accepting Jesus as his Saviour and realizing his true identity. He openly admits that he is still attracted to men but when he finds himself compelled to lust, he asks the Holy Spirit to help him overcome the temptation. At the moment of his conversion, he cut off all ties to his homosexual partners, threw out his homosexual pornography and is finding joy in celibacy. He is committed to honouring God as a single man,[l] just as he seeks to honour God in all other areas of his life. It could be that God will send him a Christian woman he finds attractive but if this doesn't happen, he is content because his primary union is with Christ. In this regard, he understands the secret apostle Paul also discovered, that of "being content in any and every situation ... through him [Jesus] who gives me strength."[m]

These two profiles demonstrate that it is the heart of the individual that matters. The Christian church as a whole needs to stop marking the individual who has experienced same-sex attraction as flawed. Rather, we need to affirm them as the child of God they are. When we do this, we encourage them to accept their *true* identity. This allows them to be freed from a gay identity, which is a lie. Does this mean they will never again experience same-sex attraction? Not necessarily, but they are given new eyes to see that like all of us, their struggle does not have to be their identity.

---

[l] See 1 Corinthians 7 for Paul's discussion on the benefits of being a single Christian in ministry.
[m] Philippians 4:12-13; For more on this topic, I recommend Caleb Kaltenbach's book, *Messy Grace*, (Colorado Springs: Waterbrook Press, 2015).

In the process of my research, I have read and viewed so many stories of men and women who were freed *from* the "lie-dentity" of homosexuality *to* their true identity in Christ. These experiences are not a result of homosexual conversion therapy or something similar. This is what happens when a person comes to identify with Jesus in a way that is infinitely more important and authentic than the homosexual identity they had adopted.

Doing What I Hate to Do

Let's again apply the theme of marriage to our identity experience. Followers of Christ are often called his bride[n] and so it is natural that when we come to Jesus we follow the biblical example for marriage in "forsaking all others." In essence, we are born joined to our sin nature,[o] identifying fully with sin – married to it even. In essence, we are born joined to our sin nature, identifying fully with sin – married to it even! Throughout our lives, we may assume additional sin identities that we are drawn into through our union with our sin nature. When we come to Christ, our sin nature or sin identity dies. We cannot go back to that relationship because the other partner is dead! We are widowed from sin and married to Christ. Attempting to return to sin is a betrayal of our new relationship with Christ.

As a Christian, I *cannot* choose identities that contradict my status as a forgiven, adopted child of God and disciple of Jesus. These two things are incompatible. It doesn't work. I can choose to identify with Christ or to identify with sin but not both.

Understanding the difference between living in sin and living in Christ is an ongoing theme in the New Testament for all believers. Paul spells it out for us in Romans:

---

[n] This is a New Testament theme, see 2 Corinthians 11:2; Ephesians 5:25-27; Revelation 19:7-9; 21:1-2.
[o] Psalm 51:5

> I do not understand my own actions. For I do not do what I want, but I do the very thing I hate ... I have the desire to do what is right, but not the ability to carry it out. For I do not do the good I want, but the evil I do not want is what I keep on doing. Now if I do what I do not want, it is no longer I who do it, but sin that dwells within me.[p]

And so, the struggle against sin is *not* just a message for those with same-sex attraction or confusion about their gender. No matter what our sin struggle, no matter how the imprint of original sin shows up in our lives, we need to choose Christ on a daily basis. Like the husband who is careful not to let his eyes wander in order to honour his marriage, we need to recognize that any time we allow ourselves to wander casually into sin we put an obstacle in our relationship with the Lord. Is there a lie-dentity that has taken hold in your life?

The Lord Jesus instructs us that being his disciple requires ongoing, daily commitment to endure trials and temptation but there is hope.

> "Then he said to them all: 'Whoever wants to be my disciple must deny themselves and take up their cross daily and follow me. For whoever wants to save their life will lose it, but whoever loses their life for me will save it.'"[q]

Maybe you have never realized the need to identify with Christ in a way that is intentional and all encompassing. It's as simple as telling him that through his power you want to put your sin nature to death and identify fully with him. Through his sacrificial death

---

[p] Romans 7:15-20, ESV
[q] Luke 9:23-24

on the cross, you can know freedom from sin and new, abundant life through him.[r]

---

[1] "Identity" (Merriam-Webster), accessed January 25, 2017, https://www.merriam-webster.com/dictionary/identity.
[2] "Stories," *Living Out*, accessed January 31, http://www.livingout.org/stories.
[3] Daly, "Navigating Sexual Sin."
[4] Ontario, Ministry of Education, *Ontario Curriculum, Grades 1-8: Health, 216*.
[5] "Session 2 Aspirations: Becket" in *Better: How Jesus Satisfies the Search for Meaning*, produced by Tim Chaddick and Craig Borlase, (2014; Los Angeles, CA: David C. Cook Studio, 2014), DVD.
[6] Ibid.
[7] Amy L. Hequembourg and Ronda L. Dearing, "Exploring Shame, Guilt, and Risky Substance Use among Sexual Minority Men and Women," *Journal of Homosexuality*, 60, no. 4, (2013:615–638), https://www.ncbi.nlm.nih.gov/pmc/articles/PMC3621125/.
[8] Maurice N. Gattis, Michael R. Woodford, and Yoonsun Han, "Perceived Interpersonal Discrimination and Depressive Symptoms among Sexual Minority Youth: Is Religious Affiliation a Protective Factor?," *Archives of Sexual Behavior*, 43, no. 8, (2014: 1589–1599), https://www.ncbi.nlm.nih.gov/pmc/articles/PMC4507415/.
[9] Ibid.

---

[r] For more information about how to become a Christian and discover your true identity in Christ, visit our website at mychildmychance.com.

Chapter 4

Our True Identity in the Chaos of Gender

"So God created man in his own image, in the image of God he created them; male and female he created them."

Genesis 1:27

I want to start this chapter with the conclusion – the bottom line. The battle over gender, the tension between the lie-dentity and our biblical identity is, at its root, *a spiritual battle*. All lies have their source in the father of lies and this one is no different.

It is easy to miss that point in all the psycho-babble. Without Jesus, *all* people are living lives that are far less than the abundant life that he desires for them.[a]

---

[a] John 10:10

Identity and Gender

Earlier we looked at the Genderbread Person, which represents the thinking of the world that each person has the freedom to identify as any gender or sexuality depending on their feelings and preference (which, in some cases, can vary by day). This model says, "I feel like I might be something other than my biological gender. It's okay because that is a normal part of the human experience. You just need to accept it ... and please do call me by my preferred pronoun!"

People who buy into this idea have believed a lie about a central part of their identity: their gender. Instead of recognizing the value of the sex they were born with and identifying accordingly, they've divorced themselves from that identity. In so doing, they have rejected an important gift God has given them, one that they have failed to recognize as such.

The wide-open options of the Genderbread model enable confusion. In contrast to that, I believe that we need to recognize that God is not the author of confusion but order.[b] The shame that often comes with gender confusion is not surprising because the Bible regularly couples confusion with shame.[c]

Everyone has specific weak points where they are especially vulnerable to temptation. Remember: Being tempted is not sin. Jesus himself was tempted by the devil but was without sin. It is when we indulge the temptation and do not follow Jesus' example in rejecting it, that we begin down the path toward sin. James 1:15 reminds us that "after desire has conceived, it gives birth to sin; and sin, when it is full-grown, gives birth to death." Based on the Word of God, we must acknowledge that gender confusion is a temptation that can lead to sin. It's *not* sinful to struggle with your gender, but

---

[b] 1 Corinthians 14:33
[c] Psalms 35:26, 40:14, 70:2, 71:24

it *can become* sin if you indulge that struggle and allow it to consume you. This is the acceptance of the lie-dentity.

Talking about gender confusion can be particularly hard because this confusion may begin at a young age. Earlier, we introduced the idea that young children can express a desire to be the other gender. This may be seen as proof for those who support transitioning a person from one gender to the other; that such a change is in the child's best interest to reduce stress and trauma from feeling dissatisfied or at odds with their gender.

Children who struggle with their gender almost always outgrow this by the time they reach adolescence – up to 98% do![1] So how can we help these kids in the meantime? I firmly believe we need to do away with the lie that they might be better off if they transition and recognize the struggle for what it is: part of a spiritual battle for the child. For starters, let's consider this passage from Philippians:

> I have told you before, and now tell you again even with tears, many live as enemies of the cross of Christ. Their destiny is destruction, their god is their stomach, and their glory is in their shame. Their mind is set on earthly things.
>
> But our citizenship is in heaven. And we eagerly await a Saviour from there, the Lord Jesus Christ, who, by the power that enables him to bring everything under his control, will transform our lowly bodies so that they will be like his glorious body.[d]

Understand that a fixation on gender is a fixation on the physical. The body is an earthly shell that is not permanent at all. I don't mean to be simplistic but it will certainly help if we can grasp the truth that there is more to life – to eternal life – than our bodies in the here and now. Jesus affirms this when he says, "Flesh gives

---

[d] Philippians 3:18-21

birth to flesh, but the Spirit gives birth to spirit. You should not be surprised at my saying, 'You must be born again.'"[e]

As believers, we need to live as if life is about more than our earthly bodies. Our bodies can be a significant distraction. If our bodies become an obsession I believe they can be used as a trick of the enemy, keeping our eyes off our Saviour and on ourselves. This goes not only for those who are consumed with thoughts of their gender but those who struggle with other elements of body image. Let's not forget that God created us in his image[f] and declared us – including our bodies – "very good"![g]

As parents we know how *foolish*, stubborn, and misled our children can be. It is our responsibility to be the voice of reason and to speak the truth into their lives. It is imperative that we teach our children what gender confusion truly is and counteract the lies the enemy is telling them.

I believe that the root of gender confusion is *jealousy*. Later we'll give some advice on how to nurture your child's God-given gender, but for now, let's look into how jealousy is at play in the mind of a gender-confused individual.

The Role of Jealousy in Gender Confusion

Jealousy, and its synonym envy, is a longing or yearning to have something that someone else has. It is the opposite of contentment, which is set up in the Bible as an ideal to strive toward. The apostle Paul says, "I have learned to be content whatever the circumstances," and tells us that the secret of contentment is through Jesus who gives us strength[h] to be content in all things. He gives us further encouragement when he writes in Hebrews to "be content with

---

[e] John 3:6-8
[f] Genesis 1:26-27
[g] Genesis 1:31
[h] Philippians 4:11-13

what you have because God has said, 'Never will I leave you; never will I forsake you.'"[i] Do not miss the promise in these passages! When we are tempted to be discontent or jealous, our source of strength and ability to overcome is through Jesus. The very presence of God is with us. We are not alone.

Although jealousy might seem like a private, minor sin that doesn't hurt anyone, we need to think again: "For where you have envy [jealousy] and selfish ambition, there you find disorder [confusion] and every evil practice."[j] This passage points out that jealousy goes hand in hand with confusion and evil.

In other passages, we are reminded that jealousy is fruitless and inappropriate for a believer.[k] It is listed as an "act of sin" alongside drunkenness and orgies.[l] When we look at jealousy in these contexts it becomes clear that it's not so minor after all, and the temptation to be jealous cannot be nurtured.

The Bible says that "a heart at peace gives life to the body, but envy rots the bones."[m] How true this is for a person who is at odds with their gender: their source of envy *is* the body. They have no peace with the bodies they were given, and tragically, if they continue to allow envy to fester, it could end up as *actual death* to parts of their bodies (in the case of surgical transition).

Having a sense in my spirit that jealousy plays a significant role in the transgender experience, I wanted to find out if anything had been written on this topic. It turned out there were a number of sources online, including a transfemale who is documenting his/her transition on YouTube saying, "For me, jealousy is the number one

---

[i] Hebrews 13:5
[j] James 3:16. Words in brackets added for clarity.
[k] Romans 13:13; 2 Corinthians 12:20
[l] Galatians 5:19-21
[m] Proverbs 14:30

indicator of being trans."[2] Other posters agreed that jealousy was a common experience for transgendered people.

The search also took me to a blog post on *transgenderreality.com*, a website whose aim is to show the real face of transgenderism. I was not prepared for what I found.

The post was entitled, "I'm a Woman Now, but I Really Hate Women Sometimes" and shares the experience of transwomen with jealousy. The article opens with, "It's not uncommon for transgender people, especially those wanting to transition to female, to be jealous and angry at women, for having what they desperately want. Sometimes, it gets ugly."[3] The blog post shared the following expressions from transwomen:

- "My lust for girls is completely intertwined with jealousy."
- "In two years, no real decline in envy. If anything, it arguably got worse ... Basically, the further along I go, the more I'm jealous of cis[n] women for being born into a place I can't ever get to."
- Another transfemale reports the reaction to meeting a 23-year-old girl who "got the life I always wanted. The princess bedroom. The prom dress. Seeing her is such a trigger for me ... I get so angry ..."
- "I can't look at nude photos of cis women if their nether region is showing ... the sight of a vagina just fills me with sadness, jealousy, and rage ... "
- "I get triggered every time I need the lady's room."[4]

This doesn't sound like a minor problem, does it? Identifying as a transgendered person does not appear to eliminate the jealousy; it can even amplify it. This lie-dentity leads to destruction and shame.

---

[n] *Cis* is a word used in the transgendered community to mean a person whose mind agrees with their body about their gender identity.

The apostle Paul speaks of this situation in Philippians: "Their destiny is destruction, their god is their stomach, and their glory is in their shame. Their mind is set on earthly things."[o] For this discussion, we can easily substitute "stomach" with "gender" or "sexuality".

Now, please know I'm not sharing this to point the finger at people who experience gender dysphoria and to showcase their struggle. I'll be honest, when I read this blog post, I cried. I cried for the people who wrote these posts and how far they are from true peace and happiness. I cried for our culture which cannot understand that enabling this confusion is destroying lives. And finally, I cried for me because sometimes I honestly feel like I just can't handle one more minute of this research. I am heartbroken.

Without Christ, our natural focus is on the wrong thing, the material. The passage in Philippians goes on to contrast this ungodly focus with the hope and anticipation of the believer: "Our citizenship is in heaven. And we eagerly await a Saviour from there, the Lord Jesus Christ, who, by the power that enables him to bring everything under his control, will transform our lowly bodies so that they will be like his glorious body."[p]

There's nothing wrong with our bodies that God's resurrection power won't fix!

The body we are in right now should not be our focus because it's not the end product. Our final body is going to be glorious and heavenly, like Jesus' body. Therefore, conversation with and about individuals who are gender-confused should focus on the need for a Saviour. And if they are believers already, that they would recognize the truth of their heavenly citizenship, praying for their minds to be renewed.[q] The struggle with body image is something that

---

[o] Philippians 3:19
[p] Philippians 3:20
[q] Romans 12:1, 2

never fully goes away for some believers. What we are suggesting here is that the Holy Spirit's work in our lives will empower us to resist the temptation to fixate on our bodies.

God has a plan for each person and that includes their gender, so let's explore God's intention behind creating the two genders.

Created for a Purpose – Including Our Gender

Since the very beginning, there have been obvious differences between the sexes. The first chapter of the Bible outlines how the two genders came to be. "So God created man in his own image, in the image of God he created him; male and female he created them."[r] It is our *gendered* selves that are created in God's image. A female reflects God's image in ways that are unique and distinct from a male.

As the creation account unfolds,[s] it becomes clear that there is a distinct design and purpose for male and female. First, God creates the man Adam and gives him the task of working in the garden and caring for it. After the Fall, this becomes working the ground, dealing with weeds and thistles and so on. When God creates the woman Eve, he gives her the role of helping the man and bearing children. It is important to note that God gave men and women distinct roles from the beginning.

Many studies have affirmed the bodily differences of the sexes. One noted that men have on average ten times more testosterone than women.[5] Another showed that women use a vocabulary that is different enough from men's to be "statistically significant."[6] Dr. Louann Brizendine, neuropsychiatrist and author of New York Times bestseller *The Female Brain* relates this story about the differences between boys and girls.

---

[r] Genesis 1:27
[s] Genesis chapters 2 and 3

One of my patients gave her three-and-a-half-year-old daughter many unisex toys, including a bright red fire truck instead of a doll.

She walked into her daughter's room one afternoon to find her cuddling the truck in a baby blanket, rocking it back and forth saying, "Don't worry, little truckie, everything will be all right."

This isn't socialization. This little girl didn't cuddle her "truckie" because her environment molded her unisex brain. She was born with a female brain, which came complete with its own impulses. Girls arrive already wired as girls, and boys arrive wired already as boys. Their brains are different by the time they're born, and their brains are what drive their impulses, values, and their very reality.[7]

These examples represent a list that could go on and on. Answers in Genesis, a Christian apologetics organization, makes this statement:

Our manhood or womanhood is not incidental; it has been given us by God as a gift ... Men and women are one "kind" (1 Corinthians 15:39), but we are not the same. This is true in several respects. As Scripture indicates and common sense shows, men and women are different anatomically. Adam named his wife "woman" because she was distinct from him, a man (Genesis 2:23). Only a man can provide the raw material by which to procreate; only a woman can bear children and nurse them.[8]

Our gender is a specific, intentional tool that we need to fulfill the purpose God has set out for us. Ephesians 2:10 (NLT) states: "For we are God's *masterpiece*. He has created us anew in Christ Jesus, so we can do the good things he planned for us long ago." We recognize a "masterpiece" as having complete, perfect fulfillment of the artist's design. When a person who has gender confusion or dysphoria takes on an identity that is contrary to the gender God gave them, they are rejecting the masterpiece God created them to be.

This isn't God's plan. He has set us up for success, giving us what we need to accomplish our purpose.[t]

At conception, God stocks our "tool-kit" with a physical body (including gender), personality, natural gifts and talents, and most importantly, our soul. Each piece of our unique design has been carefully crafted and each person is given specific strengths and challenges. At this point, we receive our physical life, but until we receive Christ, we are spiritually dead.

At salvation, we are "re-created" spiritually and given new spiritual life and new gifts which fully equip us to fulfill our original purpose. These are added to what we are given at birth. Jesus calls the beginning of our new life in Christ the "abundant life" – "I am come that they might have life, and that they might have it more abundantly."[u]

As we mature in our faith, we learn how to make the most of these unique tools so we can bring maximum glory to God. This is the ultimate fulfillment of our purpose: the glory and magnification of the name of God through our lives. It's not about us. It's all about him. This realization puts our body image struggles into context, doesn't it?

The concept that God created us with a specific purpose and intent that we can only achieve through Christ is part of the foundation that we need to instill in our children from the youngest age. Denying our gender is to cut off access to one of the tools that God has given us to fulfill our purpose! On the flip side, accepting and embracing our gender will help us to live a life that points to the character of God: his wisdom in perfect design; his immutability in not changing his mind; and his foreknowledge of what each person needs in order to accomplish their heavenly to-do list.

---

[t] 2 Peter 1:3
[u] John 10:10 (KJV)

The truth is, we can appreciate our own unique expression of masculinity or femininity – even when it contradicts gender **stereotypes** – while accepting our biological gender as the good gift it is. The masculinity and femininity spectrums show us how.

The Masculinity and Femininity Spectrums

We know that being gender confused is not God's design or plan for any person, but what can we do when someone doesn't meet gender stereotypes? We recognize and affirm the variety within each gender – that boys can be athletic, aesthetic, or anywhere in between and girls can range from dynamic to dainty. We affirm this person in their God-given gender.

In my search to clarify this idea, I came across an alternate model of gender identity that allows for the diversity we see within each gender. It has helped me immensely in understanding gender as I believe God intended it. To the best of my knowledge, this concept was first introduced by Sue Bohlin of *Probe Ministries* in 2011.[9] In this model, each of the two genders has a spectrum of its own and a person's gender is based on two separate continuums: one for female and one for male. When a child is born, God chooses where on the male or female spectrum he intends them to be for his purpose, glory, and delight. These spectrums are aptly titled the Femininity Spectrum and the Masculinity Spectrum.

> **Accepting and embracing our gender will help us to live a life that points to the character of God.**

Reflect on the diagram following which compares the same individual on the Genderbread Person continuum and the Femininity Spectrum. Based on pre-conceived assumptions, the same person can either choose to identify as "gender independent/creative/expansive or transgender" *or* as a female, who is inclined toward more tomboyish behaviour or a strong personality.

MY CHILD, MY CHANCE

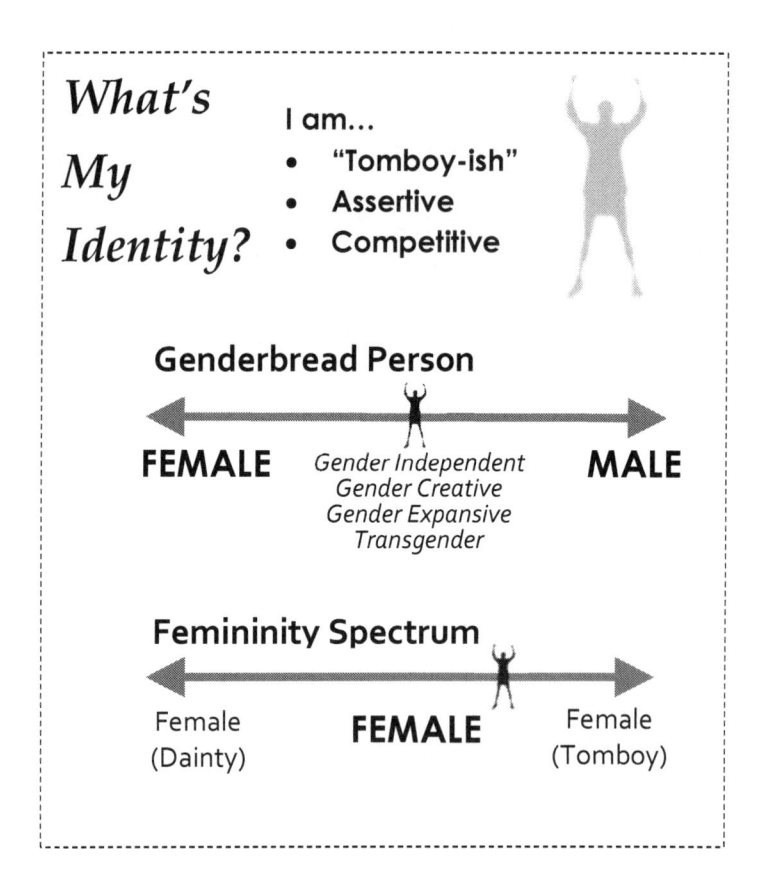

> ## What's My Identity?
>
> I am...
> - "Tomboy-ish"
> - Assertive
> - Competitive
>
> **Genderbread Person**
>
> ⬅————————➡
> **FEMALE** *Gender Independent* **MALE**
> *Gender Creative*
> *Gender Expansive*
> *Transgender*
>
> **Femininity Spectrum**
>
> ⬅————————➡
> Female   **FEMALE**   Female
> (Dainty)   (Tomboy)

The Femininity Spectrum

On one end of the Femininity Spectrum we have the dainty girl who is all about pink frills, nail polish, and ballerinas; and on the other end is the "tomboy," who can't stand any of those things and wants to play in a more "rough and tumble" way. The reality is that girls can be anywhere on this continuum and still be totally female because that's how God designed them.

A girl who veers toward the "tomboy" end may grow up feeling insecure about her femininity. She might judge herself or be judged by others to be less feminine. She could even become the target of bullying and derogatory labels.

If a girl like this does not understand that God makes girls of all types, and does not learn to see her gender, personality, and character traits as gifts or tools that are equipping her to complete the tasks God has given her to do, then she may be at risk for gender confusion or dysphoria. In the classroom or even at home, she may be drawn into confusion over her gender.

LaVern

LaVern Vivio would know. She spent her childhood and well into her adolescence wondering if God made a mistake when he made her a girl. She grew up being considered a "tomboy" because of her build. She writes:

> I suppose it was probably easier to be a 'tomboy' rather than a 'girlie' or 'sissy' guy but maybe not. Just like the guys opposite me, I was having trouble finding comfort in what God made me to be. But that was part of the journey he had for me. It's a journey I am thankful was accompanied by parents, peers, and mentors that taught me God does not make mistakes.
>
> Life was very difficult at times and the scars of adolescent taunts, a very low self-esteem, and deep, deep loneliness took its toll for many years ...

LaVern goes on to share her concern for our society where the portrayal of gender is becoming more and more confusing. In her words, the message of the culture is "to recreate our lives into what we want them to be rather than what God created us to be." She continues,

> The road we are paving for our children is so confusing and hard and it doesn't have to be ...
>
> I had a conversation with a co-worker just last year. I was concerned about my inability to connect with a couple of the women I was working with. I told him I could not understand why they

seemed to not like me, why they almost seemed uncomfortable around me. His response still makes me laugh. He said, "Well LaVern, you're basically a dude!"

So still, as basically a dude, I am completely and fully a girl, a woman. Fully and completely comfortable with who and what God made me to be.

I still detest dressing like a woman. I hate dresses and frills. I spend as much time as possible in my favorite muck boots and weathered tattered clothes working outside, getting as dirty as possible. I love working with my hands till they are rough and worn. I'm proud my hands look like hands that work, not like a man but like a woman. A woman that may be a bit rough around the edges but make no mistake, still one-hundred percent woman.

The woman God made me to be.[10]

Women in Scripture

We see within Scripture many examples of women from all over the Femininity Spectrum. Examining these women will help us to understand how God defines "female."

Consider the biblical story of Deborah and Jael.[v] Deborah was a judge and a prophetess. Barak was Israel's war captain on the battlefield against Sisera, commander of a Canaanite army. Deborah told Barak that God had promised him victory over Sisera. However, Barak, the "man" of the situation, refused to go into battle without Deborah, even with God's assurance of victory. In this battle, Sisera escaped, only to be killed by the woman Jael. She gained his confidence, lured him to sleep, and killed him by driving a tent peg through his temple with a hammer! As Deborah told Barak before

---

[v] Judges 4

the battle, "You will receive no honor in this venture, for the Lord's victory over Sisera will be at the hands of a woman."[w]

Don't forget Abigail,[x] whose shrewd wisdom countered her husband's deadly foolishness. The book of Ruth introduces us to a woman who tenderly provides for her widowed mother-in-law through hard field labour but was still beautiful enough – inside and out – to capture the attention of the rich landowner, Boaz. The book of Esther follows the life and struggles of a true "beauty queen," whose timidity required multiple attempts before she could ultimately, fearfully, fulfill the task laid before her. These women range all over the Femininity Spectrum in their display of strength, leadership, wisdom, brute force, tenderness, courage, and beauty. Each uniquely fulfilled their role in executing God's plan and purpose for their lives while not forsaking their identity as a woman.

And this is not to overlook the Proverbs 31 woman. Ever the example of Biblical perfection and the model for godly women, she exhibits character traits from all over the Femininity Spectrum. She is "energetic and strong, a hard worker" and "clothed in strength and dignity."[y] She is a wise, kind, industrious, charitable business woman without a weak bone in her body. We do not doubt her femininity for a moment and yet there is no questioning her strength either. No, there is no cause for gender identity confusion when a woman is strong, athletic, or gets great satisfaction from hard work. God has made it clear that the Proverbs 31 woman, along with Deborah and Jael, are just as gloriously feminine as Esther and Ruth.

The Masculinity Spectrum

The range of the Masculinity Spectrum is from the *athletic* — the rough-housing, sports-minded boy, who enjoys getting dirty — to

---

[w] Judges 4:9
[x] 1 Samuel 25
[y] Proverbs 31:25

the *aesthetic* boy – sensitive, gifted in the arts, music, and everything in between. As with women, Scripture affirms men at every point on the spectrum.

Men in Scripture

Was there ever a more testosterone-driven man than Samson?[z] Violent and passionate, he threw himself into hand-to-hand combat with lions and Philistines alike. Contrast him with David[aa] the gentle shepherd who spent his afternoons tenderly caring for his flock and writing Psalms. This same David was a gifted warrior, courageous giant-slayer, loyal friend, and leader of men. His passions led him both into adultery and to the generous, gentle care of an enemy's crippled grandson.

Our Lord Jesus himself demonstrates the full range of the Masculinity Spectrum. On the one hand, he tenderly provides for his mother even while dying on the cross.[bb] He welcomes and blesses the little children who come to him,[cc] grieves over Jerusalem,[dd] and reaches out in compassion to the childless widow.[ee] Time and again, he demonstrates compassion on the multitudes, the diseased, and the demonized. And yet, he did not hesitate to assert himself in judgment. In a holy rage, Jesus overturns the money-changers tables in the temple[ff] and boldly condemns the hypocrisy of the Pharisees. In the ultimate example of bravery and strength, he bore the sin of the world and silently endured the torture of the cross.

---

[z] Judges 13-16
[aa] 1 Samuel 16 to 2 Samuel 23
[bb] John 19:25-27
[cc] Matthew 19:13-15
[dd] Matthew 23:37-39
[ee] Luke 7:11-15
[ff] Luke 19:45-46

True Diversity

If these examples are not enough, when we look around at our family, friends, acquaintances, and colleagues, it should be evident that God did not create all males out of one cookie cutter and all females out of another. He created each individual in his image, and in our own unique way, we reflect the character of who he is.

This is diversity as it is meant to be celebrated! In his infinite creativity and imagination, he has designed male and female not to be rigid and limited in expression but with a wide range of personalities and possibilities. While some characteristics of male and female may overlap (i.e., a girl may be athletic and strong, and so may a boy; a boy may be sensitive and artistic, and so may a girl), the differences inside them still define them as boy or girl. The key point is that there is variation *within* each of the two genders but the differences *between* them are greater.[11] What freedom and love God has shown us: to be true to our gender, while also being completely true to ourselves.

> What freedom and love God has shown us: to be true to our gender, while also being completely true to ourselves.

Isn't it incredibly affirming to note that Scripture specifically states, whether male or female, that God's priority is the condition of the heart? God lays out his expectations for women saying, "Don't be concerned about the outward beauty of fancy hairstyles, expensive jewelry, or beautiful clothes. You should clothe yourselves instead with the beauty that comes from within, the unfading beauty of a gentle and quiet spirit, which is so precious to God."[gg]

God clarifies his priorities with respect to men when Samuel was searching for Israel's king. "The Lord said to Samuel, 'Don't judge

---

[gg] 1 Peter 3:3, 4

by his appearance or height, for I have rejected him. The Lord doesn't see things the way you see them. People judge by outward appearance, but the Lord looks at the heart.'"[hh]

The Parents' Role in Affirming Gender

As infants, children are not initially aware of being a boy or a girl but parents help their child come to appreciate their gender as they develop. It is our responsibility to recognize, affirm, and develop our children's God-given gender. My good friend Kim, also the mother of two boys, shares her experience in raising two very different sons:

> When I was expecting my second child, I remember being convinced that the child I was carrying was a girl. Everything about my pregnancy was different from my first: how sick I was, how I carried the baby, how my body changed, everything.
>
> So imagine my surprise when on delivery day, the doctor and nurses congratulated us on the birth of our second boy. I remember my shocked response being, "It's a boy ... and he has red hair!" (Red hair doesn't run in our family). Throughout my pregnancy, I knew that this child I was carrying was different from my first, and this has continued to be true as he has grown.
>
> Although our boys are very different from each other and their dad, this does not mean in any way that any one of them is less "male." God does not make mistakes. These precious children are exactly who God has created them to be.
>
> As their parents, we need to be in tune with this and to encourage and guide them in fulfilling their purpose by speaking truth into them about their identity as found in Christ. We need to recognize that the culture may try to counter this truth with lies as they see

---

[hh] 1 Samuel 16:7

fit, and be prepared to remind our sons as often as necessary that they are accepted, chosen, and beloved of God, created in His image, and that He delights in them.

Parents play a significant role in the development of their child's sense of gender. How a parent responds if their child engages in behaviours or preferences that do not conform to gender stereotypes, goes a long way toward the mental health and life outcomes for that child.

A 1986 study by Dr. Richard Green sheds some light on factors that make a difference for the more effeminate boy. The study followed boys with an ongoing lack of interest in rough-and-tumble play or other "typical" boyhood interests, and drew links between common childhood experiences and homosexual or transgender outcomes. When Dr. Green began the 15-year study, his initial impression was that he was dealing with transgendered children whose parents were concerned about their effeminacy and lack of interest in common boyish activities. Many of the boys also repeatedly expressed a desire to be girls.[12] What is noteworthy is that the outcome for these effeminate boys was more often linked to homosexuality and not transgenderism. The results of this study speak to the real danger of providing hormone therapy for the purpose of medically transitioning children to the opposite gender (sometimes before the onset of puberty).

Some wise counsel can be derived from the study with respect to how parents interact with children who do not conform to typical gender norms. The study concluded that although therapy or specific child rearing methods do not guarantee an outcome, a child's acceptance of his or her gender can be encouraged, leading to positive results.[13] This means that your attention, affection and unconditional love can have an effect on your child's sexual and gender identification.

Although the study did not examine tomboy girls, some cross-applications may be made. In the following discussion, we have focussed on boys, but if you have a daughter, think about how you can affirm her femininity even if she has not-so-girly pursuits.

Express Interest and Engage

Parents, in particular fathers, can find coping with effeminate behaviour in their sons to be very difficult. Without even realizing it, fathers can withdraw from their sons. The effeminate boys in the study were more often found to be alienated from their fathers, with fathers spending less and less time with their effeminate sons as they grew older.[14]

Possible reasons for this disconnect might be the fathers' inability to find a common ground with their boys' interest or an aversion to their effeminacy. Fathers might be trying (and failing) to engage their sons in more typical male activities and being discouraged by the lack of interest. Dr. Green suggests that fathers join their sons in the boy's preferred activity. Let's envision how this could play out.

Let's say the boy is playing house and assuming a nurturing role (perhaps dressed as a mother). Instead of trying to divert the boy from the play, a father can help his son understand how fathers nurture and care for their babies, and encourage his son to envision himself as the best future father he can be. Statements such as, "You are going to be an amazing dad one day," or "I love that you are already thinking about how you can care for the family you'll have in the future," build up the boy in a way that is sensitive to his character and interests, *and* at the same time, affirming of his gender. In this way, the boy can be applauded for his caring instinct, while also being shown that men can be nurturing (that it is not a strictly female expression).

If a boy is interested in a typically female dominated activity such as dance or gymnastics, help him build up the strength and athleticism needed to succeed. Also, find positive male role models within the child's area of interest, either in the professional arena or in real life. Finding other boys with similar interests can help as well. It might be that as the son senses his father's approval of his personality and interests, he may become more receptive to the father's suggestions of other activities to try. However, this should not be an ulterior motive. Simply giving your time and attention to your child will help to build a strong relationship. How important to do so – to have a voice when your child is struggling with his identity.

Affirm and Redirect

Keep in mind that there is a balance to be achieved. As parents, we want to affirm our child's personality, character, and biological gender while redirecting our child from cross-gender play when it crosses the line. This can be delicate. The study by Dr. Green showed that:

> Many, if not most, young children - boys as well as girls - occasionally dress up in their mothers' clothes, put on makeup or jewelry, play with dolls or assume the role of the opposite sex in fantasy play, the boys in Dr. Green's study did so almost exclusively. They spurned typical boy games, rough-housing, and sports, and instead would play with Barbie dolls for hours; frequently don female clothing; and nearly always assume a female role when playing house. Many followed their mothers around the house, mimicking the mothers' activities ...
>
> Many of the parents ... directly or indirectly encouraged the cross-gender behavior. For example, photographs of the boys dressed as girls were found in many family albums of feminine boys but in none of the albums of the comparison group of masculine boys. [15]

While it is harmless for children to break some gender stereotypes through play, we should impress upon our children that they are expressing the wonderful diversity that God permits *within* their gender. In other words, they should recognize that they are playing the role of a nurturing father, not a mother; a male nurse, not a female nurse. Their dress and mannerisms should be directed to reflect the fact that they are expressing their biological gender in concert with their personal interests, and the talents and gifts that God has given them. Fill in the blanks of these affirming phrases with a gender confused child's interests: "You don't need to dress like a girl to be ____." And, "Within God's plan and design for you, you can be a boy *and* be ____."

Avoiding an overreaction to occasional exploration is wise but gentle redirection to *persistent* tendencies to cross-dress can be equally wise. We need to be aware that in fact, the Bible warns against cross-dressing and styling one's hair in such a way as to present ourselves as the opposite gender.[ii] We need to diligently encourage our children to express their personality, develop their interests, and showcase their talents to the glory of God, all the while giving him thanks for the gender he has given them.

The above discussions may be helpful for the parent of a child who does not seem to be at significant risk of developing gender dysphoria. If these suggestions do not seem to make a change in the way your child views his or her gender, then please make every effort to seek counsel for yourself and your child. As I previously noted, it is now illegal in the province of Ontario for professionals to counsel children with gender dysphoria in any regard other than to support the child's desire to engage in opposite-sex behaviour. You may have difficulty finding help in your area but organizations such as *Focus on the Family* or your local church can be a good place to start.

Speak Truth

Scripture says, "Start children off on the way they should go, and even when they are old they will not turn from it."[jj] This takes on a whole new meaning when we consider the full spectrum of masculine and feminine behaviour. Because the expression of gender is in

---

[ii] Deuteronomy 22:5, 1 Corinthians 11:14, 15
[jj] Proverbs 22:6

part a social construct built on stereotypes (e.g., little girls in a certain culture typically wear certain clothes or like certain colours, as do little boys), individuals at the "tomboy" end of the female spectrum or the "sensitive" end of the male spectrum may be more open to the suggestion that they are lesbian, gay, or transgendered. We need to recognize this and be ready to help a child who is at risk of being lied to about his or her identity because they are presenting at the "wrong end" of their gender spectrum.

The culture, and yes, our schools, will be quick to assert the exact opposite of what we are affirming. The message will be that if a child is a tomboyish girl or a sensitive boy, they have wide-open options for their gender identity. The confusion will come at that child fast and hard in the form of bullying by peers, well-meaning encouragement, anti-homophobia instruction at school, and exposure to various media. It is virtually impossible to shelter children from these realities but ongoing teaching and validation that we are created in the image of God is vital to guiding your child's identity.[kk]

The key message for parents to deliver is that their son can be himself and still be an excellent boy. Your daughter can be true to her interests and still be an incredible girl. Your children's interests or self-expression do not change their sexuality or gender. Within God's plan, they are free to be themselves and that is pretty amazing.

This is not the mindset of the culture our kids live in or of the classrooms in which they learn. Therefore, the very serious responsibility lies with Christian parents to raise their children to function within a society whose attitude toward gender and sexuality we cannot accept. I trust that this book and our subsequent series, *Created for a Purpose*, will help parents to teach their kids to think criti-

---

[kk] Focus on the Family has a good resource entitled "Empowering Parents," which can help you respond to some of the confusing messages your children may encounter. See https://focusonthefamily.webconnex.com/co-truetolerance2016.

cally and biblically, not only about these issues but about whatever they encounter. The Bible talks about critical thinking in this way: "But test everything; hold fast to what is good. Abstain from every form of evil."[ll] Test. Hold fast. Abstain.

As Christians, we are not opposed to our children learning that others may believe and act differently; in fact, doing so is to their benefit. Not only is this a reality of the world we live in but our kids need to know there are things others believe that are different from our beliefs and what the Bible teaches. They should not be afraid to encounter these types of challenges. They should know that the Bible can hold up to scrutiny and be able to study it in order to discern what God has to say. "Do your best to present yourself to God as one approved, a worker who does not need to be ashamed and who correctly handles the word of truth."[mm]

We can hold to beliefs within our family without disrespecting the values of another. If our children are taught this principle well, compassion is nurtured within them as they learn to reach out to others who are separated from God because of sin.

---

[1] Margaret Wente, "Transgender Kids: Have We Gone Too Far?" *The Globe and Mail*, February 15, 2014, http://www.theglobeandmail.com/opinion/transgender-kids-have-we-gone-too-far/article16897043/.
[2] Itssosoph, *Being Transgender and Jealousy*," YouTube video, 00:25, February 19, 2016, https://www.youtube.com/watch?v=Zf9lWU9E0BM&feature=youtu.be.
[3] "'I Am a Woman Now, but I Really Hate Women Sometimes,'" *Transgender Reality: What Trans People Are Really Saying Online*, accessed January 25, 2017, https://transgenderreality.com/tag/jealousy/.

[ll] 1 Thessalonians 5:21-22, ESV
[mm] 2 Timothy 2:15

[4] Ibid.

[5] Anne and Bill Moir, *Why Men Don't Iron: The Science of Gender Studies* (New York: Citadel, 2000), 168, as quoted in Owen Strachan, "Transgender Identity—Wishing Away God's Design," *Answers in Genesis*, July 24, 2016, https://answersingenesis.org/family/gender/transgender-identity-wishing-away-gods-deign/?utm_source=facebookaig&utm_medium=social&utm_content=transgenderidentitywishingawaygodsdesign-19789&utm_campaign=20150416.

[6] Christina Sterbenz, "The Words That Are Most Known to Only Men or Women," *Slate: Business Insider*, June 23, 2014, as quoted in Strachan, "Transgender Identity—Wishing Away God's Design, " http://www.slate.com/blogs/business_insider/2014/06/23/center_for_reading_research_study_finds_different_vocabulary_words_are_known.html.

[7] Louann Brizendine, *The Female Brain* (New York: Broadway Books, 2006), 12.

[8] Strachan, "Transgender Identity."

[9] Sue Bohlin, "The Gender Spectrum," *Probe for Answers*, January 7, 2011, https://www.probe.org/the-gender-spectrum/.

[10] Lavern Vivio, "I Wished I Had Been Born a Boy," *Uturnlavern's Blog: Thoughts and Opinions from Uturn Lavern*, June 4, 2015, https://uturnlavern.wordpress.com/2015/06/04/155/.

[11] *Equipping Parents to Respond to Gender-Confusing Messages in Schools* (Colorado Springs: Focus on the Family, 2016), available from https://focusonthefamily.webconnex.com/co-truetolerance2016.

[12] Jane Brody, "Boyhood Effeminancy and Later Homosexuality," *New York Times*, December 16, 1986, http://www.nytimes.com/1986/12/16/science/boyhood-effeminancy-and-later-homosexuality.html?pagewanted=1.

[13] Ibid.

[14] Ibid.

[15] Ibid.

Chapter 5

RELIGIOUS FREEDOM: THE LESSER OF HUMAN RIGHTS

"If it is possible, as far as it depends on you, live at peace with everyone."

Romans 12:18

What would you say if your child was accused of having homophobic thoughts or behaviours and sent to "rehabilitative" counseling by their school – without your permission or knowledge? Think this couldn't happen? Think again.

In 2012, a couple of grade three Ontario public school students were looking at a poster in the school hallway. The poster showed two men holding hands, two women holding hands, and a man and a woman holding hands. The girls agreed together that, "When I grow up, I'm going to hold hands with a boy." A simple statement, innocently spoken but serious enough to land the girls in a series of anti-homophobia counseling sessions without the knowledge or approval of their parents. A teacher, having overheard their dialogue, judged it to be homophobic and followed her "duty" by reporting it to her administration.[a]

How could the school avoid their responsibility to consult the parents before taking a serious step such as counseling? The answer lies in the details of Ontario's Ministry of Education *Policy/Program Memorandum No. 145: Progressive Discipline and Promoting Positive Student Behaviour.* In this policy, children are disciplined or receive support following bullying, swearing, homophobic or racial slurs, sexist comments or jokes, graffiti, or vandalism.[1] As well, support may be called for when a student chooses to disclose private information to a teacher.

Because of the memorandum, teachers have to advise their principals if they observe anything of this nature. Principals usually notify the parents and discuss any supports that will be provided. However, parents are *not* notified if "doing so would put the student at risk of harm from a parent of the student, such that notification is not in the student's best interest."[2] Harm, in this memorandum, is further clarified to mean "physical, mental, emotional, and psychological" harm.

What constitutes "harm?" The term's rather vague meaning led this particular principal to forego the call home. Physical harm is, I believe, pretty well understood and often easier to see. But what is mental, emotional, or psychological harm? Who determines what harm is or when harm occurs or could occur?

Let's backtrack here a little and summarize the details of this story. The girls were viewing a poster and made a simple statement about their sexual identification. We can assume that along with about 95-98% of the population,[3] both of these young girls identified as heterosexual.

---

[a] This story was related to me by PEACE Ontario director Philip Lees, as shared with him by an Ontario mother and her daughter.

I would suggest that the decision not to call home had little to do with the perceived best interests of the children and everything to do with the interests of the principal (representing society in general) who wanted to impose a pro-homosexual ideology on the students.

The fear leading to the discipline of these girls was that these thoughts were homophobic or specifically, heterosexist. **Heterosexism** is defined by the Ontario Ministry of Education as "assumptions, practices, and behaviours that assume that heterosexuality is the only natural and acceptable sexual orientation."[4] However, I think we can agree that the girls in this situation were not making homophobic slurs. They were making a statement *about their own sexuality* but this was taken to be heterosexist by their teacher and principal. In my opinion, the principal determined that alerting the parents to the situation might 1) cause the parents to not allow the counseling; or 2) undo any "benefit" the girls might receive from the counseling. These outcomes would be perceived to cause them harm.

> **Allowing the expression of heterosexual preference to persist is now being defined as causing "mental, emotional, or psychological" harm to a child.**

To draw a clear bottom line: To allow the expression of heterosexual preference to persist is now being defined as causing "mental, emotional, or psychological" harm to a child.

The steps taken by the principal were guided by Policy Memorandum 145 which states that students should be referred to resources such as counselling, a sexual assault centre, Kids Help Phone, or the Lesbian, Gay, Bisexual, Transgendered Youth Line.[5] These suggested resources have made their way directly into the curriculum and will be discussed in depth when we look into "Community Partners" in chapter nine.

Human Rights Education

It's largely because of government bills and educational policy memorandums, built up from provincial human rights codes, that the human rights and social justice elements of education curriculums are seen as untouchable. Without these lessons, how is the culture to rehabilitate students from heterosexism and homophobia, and indoctrinate them with pro-homosexual and transgendered ideologies? And yet as Walt Heyer, a former transsexual states: Parents have rights too.

> "Parents should have access to public education for their children that does not push an ideological sexual and political agenda based on a vision of the human person that many parents deeply disagree with ..."[6]

When Instruction Becomes Indoctrination

Our human rights in Ontario are defined by the Ontario Human Rights Code. The aim of the Code is to "recognize the dignity and worth of every person and to provide for equal rights and opportunities without discrimination." It also aims to create a "climate of understanding and mutual respect."[7]

> What is lacking is the understanding that children can be instructed in these principles without having to accept practices or lifestyles which contradict their religious beliefs. Truly, insisting upon this acceptance is **indoctrination.** However, a Toronto District School Board (TDSB) document makes it clear that acceptance is mandatory:
>
> Q: Can a parent have their child accommodated out of human rights education based on Religious Grounds?
>
> A: No. "Religious accommodation" in the TDSB is carried out in the larger context of the secular education system. While the TDSB works to create a school system free from religious discrimination,

this freedom is not absolute ... For example, if a parent asks for his or her child to be exempted for any discussions of LGBTQ family issues as a religious accommodation, this request cannot be made because it violates the Human Rights Policy ... [8]

It is no longer enough to merely respect the differences in others. Students now must see all orientations and identities to be morally and socially equal. In human rights education, learning about the various grounds which are protected against discrimination is a primary strategy in addressing bullying and harassment.

Continuum of Human Rights Education

INSTRUCTION (Unbiased)	INDOCTRINATION (Religious Fervour)
Focus: The dignity and worth of all human beings through character education.	**Focus**: Eliminating homo- and trans-phobia alongside racism, classism, sexism, ableism, etc.
Result: Children who understand and respect the value of all people with heightened awareness of what makes people the *same*; children's understanding about sexual orientations and gender guided by religious values.	**Result**: Children who are hypersensitive to discrimination with heightened awareness of what makes people *different*; children accept all sexual orientations and gender identities as equally valid.
Effect on religious freedom: Respects sincerely held religious practices and beliefs.	**Effect on religious freedom:** Violates sincerely held religious practices and beliefs.

The Line

Consider the continuum of human rights education pictured above. On one side, children learn about the worth and dignity of all human beings. The goal is to create a school and a society that is "free from harassment and other forms of discrimination" by learning our rights and responsibilities.[9] On the other side is indoctrination, delivered with religious fervour, and contradicting deeply-held religious beliefs. Children are "given space" to question their sexual or gender identity regardless of their religious views on sexuality and gender. Let's be clear, manipulating students to change or abandon their religious beliefs violates their religious freedom and is an abuse of the school's authority.

Somewhere in the middle of these two models is a line where education about the worth and dignity of all people stops and indoctrination begins. We need to identify the line so that we can clearly communicate where we stand. One type of instruction we support, both at school and through our teachings at home and church, and the other we object to on a firm religious basis and want no part of for our children.

> **Manipulating students to change or abandon their religious beliefs violates their religious freedom and is an abuse of the school's authority.**

There is nothing in the Code which requires the moral approval of others' lifestyles in order to respect their dignity and worth. Rather, it is meant to govern how we treat one another, not our thoughts about others' behaviours. It would be foolish to assume that in order for everyone to be free from discrimination, everyone else must agree with all tenets of their faith, culture, or ideology. Yet this is what the culture seems to be proposing.

What Gives People Value?

When we consider the aim of the Ontario Human Rights Code, we are reminded that everyone deserves "equal rights and opportunities without discrimination."[10] Few would argue against the school's responsibility to stop discrimination and abusive behaviour between students. No student should ever be victimized: not for their sexual orientation or gender identity or for any other reason.

Since all forms of harassment are wrong, then all should be banned without distinction. Harassment, violence, and discrimination are wrong. Period. The Bible gives us many reasons to be against bullying on any level. The dignity and worth of every person is affirmed over and over again.[b] The Bible speaks out against the evils of discrimination and showing favouritism.[c] It also addresses harassment, agreeing that it should be dealt with by the courts.[d] Through Scripture, we learn that everyone is on an even platform and that when Jesus established his Church, it was on the foundation of equality.[e]

Simply being a human being, created in God's image, gives people value. This is in agreement with the Code which stresses that all people have dignity and worth.

However, wording has emerged in education documents that bears noting. We are encouraged to "value and show respect for *diversity* in the school and broader society."[11] Not for *people*, for *diversity*. There is a huge difference between honouring someone because of their diversity and honouring them because of their value.

Based on this statement, we should believe that it is one's diversity that is important rather than one's uniqueness. Please bear with me because I believe the distinction is subtle but important. Saying that you have value because of your diversity is saying, "You have more value because of the diverse elements that compose you than you would have without them." If you think this way, the more di-

---

[b] e.g., John 3:16, Matthew 7:12, Philippians 2:3
[c] James 2:1-12
[d] Matthew 5:22
[e] Galatians 3:26, 28

verse someone is, the more valuable they are, the more their opinion matters, and the more we should respect and honour them.

Elevating someone because of their diversity is the reverse of all the "isms" (sexism, racism, etc.) and in a backward way, it belittles others whose experiences or identities are more mainstream. One person's dignity and worth is increased at the expense of another's. This does not level the playing field or make the imbalance disappear. It becomes "reverse discrimination": a group that previously experienced discrimination becomes so elevated that others who do not accept the values of that group are now subject to discrimination. This is trying to make two wrongs equal a right.

There is a huge difference between honouring someone because of their diversity and honouring them because of their value.

Facing a Challenge to Your Rights and Freedoms

It's a fact that Christians and other faith groups seem to be increasingly the victims of reverse discrimination. Our values are often in conflict with the LGBT community, and now that their concerns are at the forefront, it can feel like our values are being dismissed or belittled.

Where Parents Really Stand

A Hamilton, Ontario father, Steve Tourloukis, would agree. In 2016, he went to court against the Hamilton-Wentworth District School Board over his right as a parent to know when his children would be taught about topics such as homosexuality and abortion. Justice Robert Reid of the Ontario Superior Court acknowledged that *the school board had violated the father's Charter right of religious freedom* but according to Reid, this is reasonable.

Reid concluded the board's refusal to grant Tourloukis religious accommodation, including giving him advance notice, was "reasonable," given the board's statutory obligations — particularly those outlined in the Equity and Inclusive Education Strategy launched by then-Education minister Kathleen Wynne in 2009.[12]

Considering this ruling, it is not surprising that wording in Ontario's grades 9-12 health curriculum uses phrases like "erroneous beliefs" and "misconceptions" to describe religious convictions that are in conflict with the concepts of the sexual freedom it endorses.[13] The Bible warns against allowing false teaching to infiltrate our hearts and minds: "You were running a good race. Who cut in on you to keep you from obeying the truth? That kind of persuasion does not come from the one who calls you."[f] As parents, we have a job to do when it comes to protecting our kids from those who would "cut in" on them.

I wish I could say that there is just a misunderstanding between the school system and Christian parents. We could say: "If we truly understood one another, we would see that we are on the same page with respect to discrimination and harassment." However, this is fantasy. Consider the below, published in *Diversity* magazine which is put out by the Ontario Human Rights Commission:

> *Public schools are intended to be institutions that foster tolerance and respect for diversity ...* For young children, accommodation [exemption] requests will probably be made by parents or guardians, but we should still look for opportunities to discern what students themselves want or need. The rights of the child should lie at the centre of any issue around a claim for accommodation or religious freedom, and schools must work to ensure that parental religious beliefs and rights are not operating at cross-purposes to the rights of the child. Even if we are willing to accept that parents can force their views on their children at home (or in their places of wor-

---

[f] Galatians 5:7-8

ship), we need to ensure that schools, as public institutions, are not complicit participants in this. This will obviously require walking a fine line in many cases, but such is the duty on an institution as central to our society as the school.[14]

I share this quote not to alarm you but to inform you. I firmly believe in the power of strong relationships with the staff at your child's school and so I urge you to build those relationships to ensure that your voice is heard. There is a range of adherence to these viewpoints within the system and speaking up respectfully can make a difference in forming the practice and policies of a specific classroom or even the whole school.

Be discerning. I'm not suggesting that you become paranoid – but watchful. As I said, not every school, every administrator, and every teacher is going to subscribe to these views. In our conversations, we need to be "shrewd as snakes and as innocent as doves."[g]

Know Your Rights

Parents must be aware of their rights and the rights of their children, and willing to engage respectfully when they are challenged or ignored.

The Evangelical Fellowship of Canada (EFC) has prepared a document with background and legal information for parents. Even with the ruling in the Tourloukis case mentioned previously, I believe these points stand. The document is called "Hands Up! Identifying Parents' Rights in the Education System" and is available in full on the EFC's website.[15]

Parents

It is important to know your rights and your child's rights in the school system. You have the right to determine the kind of educa-

---

[g] Matthew 10:16

tion your child will receive. Your child has the right to have his or her personal beliefs respected but might not have them respected unless you intervene. There are serious issues where morality and philosophy are being taught in schools in a way that does not respect religious differences. Parents have the right to engage on these issues.

It is valuable to make the effort to establish a good working relationship with teachers and administrators. Ask that you be advised by the teacher if subject matter is coming up that may be of concern based on your beliefs and values.[h] Keep in touch with your child about what is going on in school, especially as it regards moral and philosophical education or areas where you may feel that personal religious beliefs will not be respected in classroom instruction.

Some provinces have established a significant role for parent councils and similar parent bodies. This is a good place to get involved to help shape policy in the schools.

Students

As students, you should know your rights. You have the right to be respected in your school. And you have the right to a welcoming environment. This means that if your teacher mocks your religious beliefs, your teacher is wrong and you can challenge this to the administrators of the school (vice-principal, principal, etc.) and/or to representatives from the school board (supervisors, superintendents, trustees, etc.). You do not need to be angry or adversarial. It is important that you be respectful and that you stand up for your right to be respected in the school system.

---

[h] As per the Tourloukis case referenced earlier in the chapter, this type of request may not be honoured. However, it is my belief that parents need to continue to have a conversation with the schools, being clear about the areas where they have concern and seeking the best solution for their child's sake.

Parents of minor students may be required to engage in order for students' rights to be recognized.

Everyone

Pray for students, parents, and teachers. Pray that they will be able to find ways to have their religious beliefs and practices respected. Pray for greater inclusion of Christian education in the public school system, and greater support for private schools. Many Christians have felt excluded from the public education system yet for many the price of private schooling is prohibitively high. And pray for those who home-school. It is a challenge to teach your children, and yet it is a good way to instill Christian virtues and understanding of the world in which we live.[16]

Find Support

At some point, your rights may be challenged subtly or overtly by the school system. The form and degree of the challenge may differ from case to case but it's important to be equipped with a response for such a situation. If you feel your school has overstepped its boundaries in teaching concepts that are infringing upon your religious freedoms, *be engaged but do not be alone*. If at all possible, get support from other parents who have similar concerns. Some steps to consider:

- Talk to your pastor and solicit the support of your church as you prepare to present your concerns to the school.

- Talk to other parents from the school or community who may share the same concerns.

- Approach the school administration with a group (who will be physically present with you or have signed documentation) asking for your concerns to be considered. Come prepared with a solution to meet your children's needs. Reinforce that your children need to "see themselves reflected in the curriculum"[17] just as much as other children do.

- Do not hesitate to approach parents who are not Christians, or from other religious backgrounds. You may find support from other families who share your concerns for religious freedom and parental rights and are willing to come alongside you in addressing your concern.[i]

Consider Other Options

When I reflect on the story at the beginning of this chapter, I find myself thinking that it is unfortunate that the parents of those girls did not choose legal action. While I support the need to withdraw children from this type of situation, I also believe that there is a time to allow the legal process to take place. In my research, I regularly encountered statements that underscored how very few times religious freedoms have been tested in Canada's courts. Without these tests and court judgments, abuses will continue and spread. Here's what Bruce Clemenger, president of the Evangelical Fellowship of Canada has to say about why the EFC gets involved in court cases regarding religious freedom.

> On one hand, church leaders and individual Christians are grateful for the religious freedom we do have in Canada, especially compared to other parts of the world where it might be illegal to form a church and hold services or have educational institutions that are faith-based. We appreciate our religious freedom, we cherish it in fact, and it is right that we do. But we also must be conscientious caretakers of it. What you cherish, you protect.[18]

It's been my observation that Christians tend to shy away from the legal system, preferring to resolve conflict quickly and quietly. This can be like snapping off a weed but leaving the root in the ground. The problem may go away for your family but the root of

---

[i] For advice and practical support in this scenario, visit peaceontario.com.

the problem will cause the weed to grow again for the next family to stumble upon.

"Hands Up!" provides further guidelines and Scriptural support for Christians who may be facing a potential legal challenge.

> Paul gives some general instruction in the book of Romans just prior to the famous passage about respecting civil authority in chapter 13. He instructs: "If it is possible, as much as depends on you, live peaceably with all men." (Romans 12:18); "Do not be overcome by evil but overcome evil with good." (Romans 12:21); "Bless those who persecute you; bless and do not curse." (Romans 12:14).
>
> However, Paul used the Roman legal process when appropriate. When he had been wronged as a Roman citizen, he appealed to Caesar. And God used this for good. In Canada, we have legal processes that are for the benefit of all in our society. We can use these processes to ensure that everyone in Canada enjoys religious freedom. It is not offensive to Canadian government authority to write a letter to a politician or even to start a legal action when appropriate.[19]

As parents, we cannot afford to sit idly by when our religious freedoms and parental rights are being challenged. Nor can we run away from the fight. If we do not take a clear stand for the rights and freedoms we have today, only one thing is certain, tomorrow, we will have fewer rights and freedoms. So take courage, take up the armour of God, and take action. And most certainly, pray ... without ceasing.

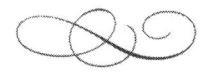

---

[1] Ontario, Ministry of Education, "Policy/Program Memorandum No. 145," 7.

[2] Ibid., 9, emphasis mine.
[3] Statistics Canada, "Canadian Community Health Survey."
[4] Ast et al., *Challenging Homophobia and Heterosexism*, 209.
[5] Ontario, Ministry of Education, "Policy/Program Memorandum No. 145," 10.
[6] Walt Heyer, "Public School LGBT Programs Don't Just Trample Parental Rights, They Also Put Kids at Risk," *The Witherspoon Institute: Public Discourse*, June 8, 2015, http://www.thepublicdiscourse.com/2015/06/15118/.
[7] Ontario, Attorney General, "Human Rights Code," 3.
[8] Ast et al., *Challenging Homophobia and Heterosexism*, 10.
[9] Ontario Human Rights Commission, "Bill 13 and Bill 14."
[10] Ontario, Attorney General, "Human Rights Code," 4.
[11] Ontario, Ministry of Education, *The Ontario Curriculum, Grades 1-8: Health and Physical Education*, 67.
[12] Lianne Laurence, "Judge Upholds Forced LGBT Indoctrination in Ontario Schools, Tells Christian Dad to Pull Kids out If He Objects," *LifeSiteNews*, November 24, 2016, https://www.lifesitenews.com/news/breaking-judge-upholds-forced-lgbt-indoctrination-in-ontario-schools-tells.
[13] Ontario, Ministry of Education, *The Ontario Curriculum, Grades 9-12: Health and Physical Education*, 126.
[14] Cara Faith Zwibel, "Faith in the Public School System: Principles for Reconciliation," in *Creed, Freedom of Religion and Human Rights - Special Issue of Diversity Magazine* 9, no 3 (*Summer 2012*): 48-51, emphasis and brackets mine, http://www.ohrc.on.ca/sites/default/files/Diversity%20Magazine_Creed_freedom%20of%20religion-human%20rights_accessible.pdf.
[15] "Hands Up!: Identifying Parents' Rights in the Education System; A Discussion Paper on Understanding the Rights and Responsibilities of Parents, Children, Education Institutions and Government" (Ottawa: The Evangelical Fellowship of Canada, October 2010), http://files.efc-canada.net/si/Education/HandsUpIdentifyingParentsRights2010.pdf.
[16] Ibid., 24-26.
[17] Ast et al., *Challenging Homophobia and Heterosexism*, 2.
[18] "A Word from the President, Bruce J. Clemenger," in *Canada Watch* (Evangelical Fellowship of Canada, January 2017), 4, http://files.efc-canada.net/efc/newsletters/canadawatch/CW2016Dec.pdf.
[19] "Hands Up!," 26.

Part 2

THE CHAOS OF SEX EDUCATION:

WHEN CHILDREN ARE TAUGHT TO ACCEPT A LIE

*"You were running a good race.
Who cut in on you to keep you from obeying the truth?"*

Galatians 5:7

Chapter 6

The Culture Comes to the Classroom

*"Their glory is in their shame.
Their mind is set on earthly things."*

Philippians 3:19

In what seemed to be an act of "damage control," the Ontario government released an advertisement in late summer 2015 touting the reasons why an update was necessary.

In the video, a boy is shown looking curiously at a wedding cake topper with two grooms; a girl fidgets with how her shirt hangs over her hips; a boy claps his hand over his mouth while looking at a computer screen; a girl begins to lift her top and position her phone for a selfie; a boy leads a girl by the hand into a house and the girl looks excited but unsure. At the end of the advertisement, each child is showing raising a hand as a voiceover says, "Our kids have questions. The sex ed and health curriculum can help. Learn more about the first update since 1998 and also how they'll help kids stay healthy and safe at ontario.ca/hpe.[1]

The message of the ad is clear: without this curriculum, our children are on their own in negotiating the tough situations we can expect them to encounter day by day.

It's hard to argue that what is shown in the ad is not commonplace because, in fact, it is. Kids need to be prepared for these situations but what is the best way to prepare them? Is the curriculum taking the best approach? What can you as a parent be doing? Start by knowing what you are up against.

The "Social Justice" Classroom

Formal learning **expectations** about sexual orientation and gender identity are a part of the health curriculum but it would be naïve to believe that instruction on these topics can only happen when they are officially in the curriculum. The timeline from chapter one highlighted that these topics have been taught for some time under the banners of social justice and human rights.

Social justice occurs when injustice is fought to promote a just and diverse society. It generally includes the "isms": racism, sexism, classism, and ableism, and has now been expanded to include heterosexism and homophobia.

At first blush, social justice sounds like a great opportunity for children to learn to think empathetically and outwardly. It is only when we look deeper that we begin to question some of the concepts that may be taught under this banner.

In 2011, four years before the release of the updated health curriculum, the Toronto District School Board consolidated a number of its anti-homophobia resources into a new document, *Challenging Homophobia and Heterosexism*. The following is a list of suggestions from the guide for teachers to implement in the class and school environment, with commentary I've added (in brackets) for clarity. Keep in mind, this is *before* the new curriculum was implemented.

- Connect discrimination based on sexual orientation and gender identity to racism, sexism, classism, and ableism (the "isms").

- Bring visitors from the LGBT community in to talk about their experiences.

- In context of a "long-term commitment to anti-homophobia," give children "time to reflect on their own ideas and values."[2] (Done under the guidance of teachers or community partners, this encourages children to adopt the values being promoted at school over those taught at home.)

- Create a prominent anti-homophobia display to acknowledge the contributions of LGBT individuals; these should also be shared every morning on the announcements throughout the school year, for example, "a short biography ... a poem, a novel excerpt highlighting the struggles and victories of LGBTQ people in Canada."[3] (It's hard to imagine a school where this recommendation would be taken literally. Such blatant preferential treatment of the LGBT community would be impossible to balance with highlights from a variety of races, abilities, people who have overcome poverty, and so forth. Nor is there any indication that such balance is the goal.)

- "Provide space for students to empower themselves to act and behave in ways that challenge homophobia and heterosexism."[4] (This is the ultimate objective: to create a generation that will actively support the LGBT community.)

Bearing all this in mind, is it any surprise to read an early-2015 news report about a Peel District School Board teacher in Mississauga, Ontario, who has operated her classroom on social justice principles since 2004?[5] This teacher explained how she would link a math lesson with social justice. Mathematically, she might be covering the measurement of the inside angles of triangles and identifying triangles by their mathematical name but the real purpose would be to communicate pro-homosexual values to her students. She could do this by connecting the lesson to the use of a pink triangle by the Nazis to shame and identify sexually deviant people, including homosexuals. This teacher related how following math, her grade 4-5 students created "badges of pride ... because that's what the pink triangle has become, it's become a symbol of pride."[6] She pointed out that parents fail to realize "just how extensive pro-LGBT issues are in the classroom and curriculum."[7]

This news story was corroborated to me by a fellow Ontario teacher (also in Peel) who overheard another teacher's lesson taking place in a nearby open-concept classroom. My friend shared how her colleague had been coaching children to disregard family values. This teacher prompted her students with the question, "What will you do if your parents say that being gay isn't okay?" and then instructed them to reply with a correcting "Tsk, tsk." In subsequent conversations with my friend, this social justice teacher shared that her methods also included teaching all the "isms" in order to freely teach her students to be pro-gay.[8]

Such is the reality of some "social justice" classrooms and it can be expected to expand in scope and breadth in the coming years. Hiren Mistry, Instructional Coordinator for Equity & Inclusive Education in the Peel District School Board, put it this way: "Equity is not an add-on; it is the foundation of everything."[9]

Anti-discrimination education has been a part of Ontario's arts curriculum since 2009. In this curriculum document, it is acknowledged that the arts provide a unique opportunity to explore positive coping mechanisms for the "social and emotional impact of various forms of discrimination, such as racism, sexism, homophobia, and religious intolerance, as well as the effects of bullying, harassment, and other expressions of violence and hatred."[10] The arts curriculum itself provides a number of expectations and further suggestions to assist teachers in making this happen:

- In dance, grade 7 students "construct personal interpretations of the messages in their own and others' dance pieces ... (e.g., dance pieces on topics such as urban sprawl, land claims, poverty, homophobia, homelessness), and communicate their responses in a variety of ways.[11]

- "Same-sex partnering and grouping should be supported, and opportunities to explore non-stereotypical social roles in dance forms should be provided."[12]

- Drawing attention to traditional and non-traditional gender and social roles in visual art materials being studied.[13]

Since social justice and anti-homophobia education have been around for some time, parents can expect their children to continue to be taught concepts that go beyond the core curriculum. Studying the curriculum, we learn what *must* be taught but we are no wiser about what *may* be taught in many classes. Already reports are coming in that girls in rural and northern Ontario schools have been told they can try a strap-on penis if they want to see what it's like to be a boy.[14] What's next?

Studying the curriculum, we learn what *must* be taught but we are no wiser about what *may* be taught.

The Goal of the Curriculum

So frequently when doing research for this book, I have thrown up my hands in frustration and wondered how the content in the sexual health curriculum will ever build healthy adults who are prepared for stable relationships.

I think this can be compared to two groups working in a kitchen, under the impression they are making the same dish. However, one group has a recipe for Red-Hot Chili and the other has a recipe for chocolate chip cookies. Until they realize they are working toward two very different results, confusion or ridicule over why the other is using different ingredients and method is to be expected.

Here's the correlation to sex education. As Christian parents, we disagree with some of the major elements of the curriculum (the ingredients) because we disagree with the end goal for our children's sexuality (the dish being prepared). Developing sexually healthy adults cannot be the goal of the curriculum. The input affects the outcome, and the desired outcome is very clear.

Dr. Miriam Grossman, a medical doctor and American expert on sexuality education, writes how she uncovered the vision for the type of sex education that is now in Ontario. When on staff at UCLA's Student Counseling Services, she witnessed "hundreds and hundreds of young people in distress due to medical issues, only to discover how esteemed health authorities give an enthusiastic thumbs-up to the very behaviours that fuel those problems."[15] She writes of the groups leading sexuality education in the USA:

> They are not about preventing disease. Sex ed is a social movement. Its goal is to change society. The primary goal of groups like SIECUS, Planned Parenthood, and Advocates for Youth is to promote sexual freedom and to rid society of its Judeo–Christian taboos and restrictions. In this worldview, almost anything goes. Each individual makes his or her sexual choices; each person decides how much risk he or she is willing to take, and no judgments are allowed.[16]

The vision that these groups have of sex education is *not* sexual health. It is sexual freedom.[17] This is a vision that is shared by those who created the Ontario curriculum.

Take note of the following philosophies about sexual health, written by key contributors to the 2015 Health and Physical Education

Curriculum[18], and consider if these philosophies represent sexual health or sexual freedom.

Toronto Public Health

> Sexuality is an important part of every human being, which includes how we act, think and feel. Healthy sexuality cannot be separated from basic human rights ... Our programs aim to promote a satisfying, safe, and pleasurable sexual life, while reducing harm, judgement, shame, guilt, coercion, and abuse.[19]

Planned Parenthood Toronto

> - Healthy sexuality is an important part of life.
> - Providing responsive, client-centred services means being pro-choice, youth-positive, woman-positive, sex-positive and lesbian, gay, bisexual, trans, queer-positive.
> - We can only identify how power and privilege play out when we are conscious and committed to understanding how racism, sexism, homophobia, transphobia, and other forms of oppression affect each one of us. [20]

Canadian AIDS Society

> Recognizing that healthy sexual attitudes and behaviours are essential to preventing transmission of HIV/AIDS, CAS promotes a sex-positive perspective. With discrimination due to homophobia and heterosexism contributing to increased risk behaviour for HIV, we encourage an open attitude towards sexuality and want people to talk about it, to embrace the joys it has to offer and to celebrate it, in all of its diverse forms.[21]

Remove Barriers to Acceptance

Introducing the topics of gender identity and sexual orientation early on goes a long way toward helping children to grow up to accept them. Robb Travers, an associate professor of Health Sciences and Psychology at Wilfrid Laurier University and an expert on LGBT youth, says there's a "huge benefit" to teaching young children that different kinds of sexuality are healthy and normal: "Children are remarkable in terms of compassion and understanding ... Most studies show that when kids are exposed to that kind of information at a young age, they don't really have any problem accepting it."[22]

I have heard numerous reports of children in kindergarten and early primary grades coming home with information about being transgender such as, "My teacher says anyone can be a boy *or* a girl!" News reports are sharing more and more about teachers who are coming out to their students or showcasing their transgender identity. A Globe and Mail article entitled "When Ms. Straughan became Mr. Straughan: How a Transgender Teacher Learned to be Himself" was shared on Facebook by the Elementary Teachers' Federation of Ontario (ETFO). The article disclosed how in the 2015-2016 school year, a kindergarten teacher has "challenged young developing minds – and a few adults – about gender labels and inclusiveness at the Hamilton-Wentworth District School Board." In the classroom, cross-gender play is encouraged. For example:

> A four-year-old boy who called himself Rohunzel, his take on the character Rapunzel, twirled around the room in a flowing gown and hair made of long strands of paper that kissed the ground. Mr. Straughan encouraged his students to try costumes over their school uniforms, to explore different characters and genders. He has enjoyed the play-based learning of kindergarten. He said he feels that he belongs – and where he believes he can have the biggest impact. It wouldn't be out of ordinary to find Mr. Straughan's teaching partner, Tyler Robertson-Roper, an early childhood education worker, wearing a skirt. 'We have the ability, as kindergarten teachers ... to just expose them to something else and to ask them why. Why can only a boy do that or why does a girl do that?' said Mr. Robertson-Roper. 'I grew up being taught that there's no

such thing as boy things and girl things. That was my household. I bring that to my teaching and to my parenting.'[23]

From kindergarten through high school, instruction on gender identity and sexual orientation prods students toward acceptance, following the mandate of Ontario's Equity and Inclusive Education Strategy of *"moving beyond tolerance to acceptance and respect."*[24]

The Ontario curriculum takes clear aim at any barriers that stand in the way of this goal. In grade 9, students are expected to "demonstrate an understanding of factors that can influence a person's understanding of their gender identity (e.g., male, female, two-spirited, transgender, transsexual, intersex, etc.) and sexual orientation (e.g., heterosexual, gay, lesbian, bisexual, etc.), and identify sources of support for all students."[25]

Major factors that contribute to this understanding are listed as acceptance, stigma, culture, religion, media, stereotypes, homophobia, self-image, and self-awareness.[26] These are systematically addressed throughout the curriculum as shown in the Appendix.

Below is a potential dialogue that could occur around this topic in a grade 9 classroom, taken from the teacher prompts and student responses within the curriculum. It is included in full in order to give you a sense of the suggested approach.

> *Teacher prompt:* "Gender identity refers to a person's sense of self, with respect to being male or female, both, or neither, and may be different from biological or birth-assigned sex. Sexual orientation refers to how people think of themselves in terms of their sexual and romantic attraction to others. What determines a person's sense of self? How do social expectations and stereotypes about gender and sexuality influence how a person may feel about their gender identity or sexual orientation?"
>
> *Student response:* "A person's sense of self is affected by the person's cultural and family background, religion, and what they have come to value. Media images, role models, support systems, and

acceptance or lack of acceptance by others could influence how different people feel about their gender identity or sexual orientation." "Expectations or assumptions about masculinity and femininity and about heterosexuality as the norm can affect the self-image of those who do not fit those expectations or assumptions. This can make it difficult for a person to feel accepted by others."

Teacher prompt: "What are some sources of support for students who may be questioning their gender identity or sexual orientation?"

Student response: "Talking to other young people dealing with the same issues can be a great start. It's important to know that you are not alone. Many communities have organizations that provide services for gay, lesbian, bisexual, and transgender youth, as well as for those who are questioning their gender identity or sexual orientation and for allies who support them. School guidance counsellors, health professionals, and trusted adults and friends can also help." "Student-led clubs, such as gay-straight alliances, can make a big difference. As individuals, we can help by always treating each other fairly and with respect. In our society, it is important to respect and accept the rights of all."

There are a couple of persistent issues with the curriculum that are evident in the prompts above. First, the question is posed: If you are *questioning* your gender identity or sexual orientation, what are some sources of support? The answer is focused on sources or community organizations that are geared toward gay, lesbian, bisexual, and transgender youth. Can you imagine the impact of referring a *questioning* (confused) teen to an LGBT community partner? What would be a likely outcome for that youth?

Another major concern is that the list of supports given in the quote above includes other LGBT young people, community organizations, school guidance counsellors, health professionals, trusted adults, and gay-straight alliances. *Parents* are never mentioned as people who could support the children when they are questioning their sexuality. Why do you think this is?

These two serious concerns surface time and again. The curriculum continually "errs" on the side of fostering homosexuality. Heterosexual outcomes are not given the same encouragement as homosexual ones. Further, the role of parents in mentoring their children is not reinforced.

The Current Reality

Clearly, the curriculum wasn't developed in a vacuum. It reflects where our culture currently stands. Parents continue to be upset and many remain convinced that the only way to fix the problem is to remove the curriculum from public schools. As much as I would like to believe that doing so would make a difference, the reality is that our children are not products merely of their school environment but also of the culture at large. More importantly however, they are products of our homes and so it is there that our dedication and commitment can have the greatest effect.

The vision that these groups have of sex education is NOT sexual health. It is sexual freedom.

Historically in North America, we have been accustomed to the culture around us being in alignment with Christian values. However, the cultural mindset is now opposed to the teachings of Christianity, particularly with respect to sexuality and gender identity. This oppositional mindset is not new to the world or history. Consider the description of the society of the apostle Paul when he wrote to the Romans:

> Claiming to be wise, they instead became utter fools ... Even the women turned against the natural way to have sex and instead indulged in sex with each other. And the men, instead of having normal sexual relations with women, burned with lust for each other. Men did shameful things with other men, and as a result of

this sin, they suffered within themselves the penalty they deserved ... They know God's justice requires that those who do these things deserve to die, yet they do them anyway. Worse yet, they encourage others to do them, too.[a]

"Encouraging others to do them, too," is the feared outcome for our children – that they would be the "others." What is being done through specific, targeted instruction within the schools is a clear example of the type of "encouragement" the Romans passage warns about. Factors or barriers to full acceptance of LGBT practices and identities, outlined in the curriculum as acceptance, stigma, culture, religion, media, stereotypes, homophobia, self-image, and self-awareness, are systemically being eliminated in the minds of our kids.

In the following chapters, we will examine these themes in detail, provide potential lesson samples from established sources, and investigate concerns that may arise.

---

[1] OnGov, *Sex Education in Ontario: Show of Hands*, YouTube video, 0:00-0:30, September 10, 2015, https://www.youtube.com/watch?v=wamYCuBYzQ4&feature=youtu.be.
[2] Ast et al., *Challenging Homophobia and Heterosexism,"* 30.
[3] Ibid.
[4] Ibid.
[5] Pete Baklinski, "Lesbian: I Use Math Class to Teach Young Kids about Homosexuality so I Can 'hide' It from Parents," *LifeSiteNews*, April 24, 2015,
https://www.lifesitenews.com/news/lesbian-i-use-math-class-to-teach-young-kids-about-homosexuality-so-i-can-h.
[6] Ibid.
[7] Ibid.
[8] Anonymous, email message to author, April 26, 2015.

---

[a] Romans 1:22-32, NLT

[9] Baklinski, "Lesbian: Math Class."
[10] Ontario, Ministry of Education, *The Ontario Curriculum, Grades 1-8: The Arts,* 50.
[11] Ibid., 137.
[12] Ibid., 50.
[13] Ibid.
[14] Phil Lees, "Kids in Northern Ontario School Told: 'Wear a Strap-on Penis,'" *PEACE Ontario Facebook Page*, September 26, 2015, https://www.facebook.com/PEACE-Ontario-358501781004633/timeline/.
[15] "About," *Miriam Grossman, MD*, accessed January 26, 2017, http://www.miriamgrossmanmd.com/about/.
[16] Miriam Grossman, "You're Teaching My Child What? The Truth About Sex Education," *Heritage*, August 9, 2010, http://www.heritage.org/research/lecture/youre-teaching-my-child-what-the-truth-about-sex-education.
[17] Miriam Grossman, *You're Teaching My Child What? A Physician Exposes the Lies of Sex Ed and How They Harm Your Child* (Washington, D.C.: Regnery Publishing, Inc., 2009), 7.
[18] Sherry Bortolotti, from of the Ontario Ministry of Education, "Response to Your Inquiry," list of contributors to the curriculum was provided in email message to author, October 30, 2015.
[19] Toronto Public Health, "Our Philosophy on Sexual Health," *City of Toronto*, 2017, http://www1.toronto.ca/wps/portal/contentonly?vgnextoid=f9e87dbbfd510410VgnVCM10000071d60f89RCRD.
[20] "Our Mission, Vision and Values," *Planned Parenthood Toronto*, accessed January 26, 2017, http://www.ppt.on.ca/about-us/our-mission-vision-and-values/.
[21] "Sexual Activities," *Canadian AIDS Society*, accessed November 4, 2015, http://www.cdnaids.ca/sexualactivities.
[22] Kathleen Jolly, "Reality Check: What's the Evidence behind Ontario's Sex Ed Curriculum?," *Global News*, March 4, 2015, http://globalnews.ca/news/1863258/reality-check-whats-the-evidence-behind-ontarios-sex-ed-curriculum/.
[23] Caroline Alphonso, "When Ms. Straughan Became Mr. Straughan: How a Transgender Teacher Learned to Be Himself," *Globe and Mail*, April 22, 2016, http://www.theglobeandmail.com/news/toronto/when-ms-straughan-became-mr-straughan-how-a-transgender-teacher-learned-to-be-himself/article29726503/.
[24] Ontario, Ministry of Education, *Realizing the Promise of Diversity*, 2.
[25] Ontario, Ministry of Education, *The Ontario Curriculum, Grades 9-12: Health and Physical Education*, 104.
[26] Ibid.

Chapter 7

UNBUCKLING THE GENDER STRAIGHTJACKET

*"Stop judging by mere appearances,
but instead judge correctly."*

John 7:24

In 1969, due to a severely botched circumcision, a boy known as John/Joan had his genitals removed and was raised as a girl. Overseeing his care was Dr. John Money of the John Hopkins Hospital, who comforted the boy's parents with his theory that gender is a "social construct." John/Joan could be raised as a girl and wouldn't know the difference.

But John/Joan did know the difference. Growing up, he was confused by his constant desire to dress and play like a boy, preferring the boyish activities his twin brother enjoyed, over the girlish activities offered to him. At the age of 15, he rejected his assigned female gender and began to live as a boy.[1] Tragically, he ultimately committed suicide,[2] but Dr. John Money's theory lives on.

In the decades since, the idea has persisted that boys and girls become their gender because of expectations that begin the moment the doctor announces their sex at birth. Despite the obvious faults in Dr. Money's theories, it is still a prevailing thought that gender identity develops primarily by the way a child is socialized – as either a boy or a girl. This theory has been a driving force behind the feminist movement: "Feminism should aim to create a 'genderless (though not sexless) society, in which one's sexual anatomy is irrelevant to who one is, what one does, and with whom one makes love.'"[3]

Nearly fifty years later, this thinking has evolved from a desire to have equality of the sexes, to questioning *whether there even are just two sexes*. The current idea is that if we can only get rid of stereotypes, then children would be able to decide what they want their gender identity to be without concern for traditional gender roles or expectations. They will be free from their "gender straightjacket."[4] This is the thrust of the curriculum regarding stereotypes.

The Barrier of Stereotypes

People are unique. We are not all formed from the same stereotypical cookie-cutter so this means that stereotypes can hurt. So says the Ontario 2015 Health and Physical Education curriculum, and I think we can all agree with that. The following is the curriculum's definition of a stereotype:

> A false or generalized, and usually negative, conception of a group of people that results in the unconscious or conscious categorization of each member of that group, without regard for individual differences. Stereotyping may be based on race, ancestry, place of origin, colour, ethnic origin, citizenship, creed, sex, sexual orienta-

tion, age, marital status, family status, or disability, as set out in the Ontario Human Rights Code, or on the basis of other factors.[5]

Like other forms of stereotyping, using generalizations such as "all boys" or "all girls" can be negative. For example, boys and girls typically handle stress differently. Girls are likely to look to others for support and protection while boys tend toward "fight or flight."[6] This means if a girl decides to fight in a difficult situation, she might be called a "butch." If a boy cries or seeks support when stressed, he might be considered "weak" or "girlie." The result of the stereotype is that a person feels like there is something "bad" or "wrong" about them because they don't fit the expected stereotype.

The fact is, not all boys are going to "fight or flight" to de-stress and not all girls are going to seek out support and protection. Applying the stereotype with a broad stroke in a way that causes people to doubt their identity or sexuality is very harmful. Obviously, this can lead to confusion, anxiety, and self-doubt.

In trying to reduce the harm caused by stereotypes, the curriculum attempts to redefine what is normal. Stereotypes get special mention in grade 6. Students "assess the effects of stereotypes, including homophobia and assumptions regarding gender roles ... on an individual's self-concept, social inclusion, and relationships with others, and propose appropriate ways of responding to and changing assumptions and stereotypes."[7]

How people see themselves *can* be damaged by stereotypes about gender and sexuality. When someone doesn't match the stereotype, it's true that others might assume that they are gay or transgendered and make comments along those lines (examples of a "homophobic" response). This can be harmful to the individual on many levels.

The solution in the curriculum has two parts. First, it suggests that you respond appropriately, a somewhat vague idea. The second action is to change assumptions and stereotypes.

It is the second part that requires caution. Which specific stereotype needs to be changed? What part of the stereotype is causing harm? How these questions get answered depends on the mindset or worldview of the person doing the answering.

The reality is that schools have taken on the mission of making everyone feel good about themselves without moral judgment over what is right or wrong. In doing so, stereotypes get thrown under the bus and are labelled "usually untrue."[8] So are they wrong? This is very tricky to unpack but stay with me as I do my best.

There are stereotypes that are unnecessary and can cause harm. With very few exceptions, we can encourage both boys and girls to ignore limiting stereotypes and enjoy whatever sport or pastime piques their interest. Likewise, boys and girls can be encouraged to aspire to any career – it's equally appropriate for both boys and girls to become a nurse or a pilot, for example. Some limits may exist because of physical differences between the sexes but there are usually exceptional men or women who can overcome these differences and succeed regardless. It's easy to see that stereotypes like these can be discarded or replaced without compromising on biblical truths.

But other "stereotypes" stem from the order that God set out in the very beginning for men, women, and relationships. Actually, these are not stereotypes at all but the natural order and God's plan. If we destroy this structure, we lose something good, foundational, and biblical. In essence, we surrender our culture to confusion and frustration.

"Normal" – A Moving Target

God has specifically set out standards and expectations for gender identity and sexual orientation. The very basic requirement for procreation and the continuation of the human species requires sexual encounters between men and women. Changing "stereotypes" about sexual orientation means that same-sex and opposite-sex relationships are presented as not only equally healthy but equally likely to occur as well.

This line of thinking says that when you ask someone about their relationship, you should not assume that they are with someone of the opposite gender because that is stereotypical and heterosexist. Encouraging the use of the terms "partner" or "spouse" in place of "husband" or "wife" is one step toward eliminating this so-called stereotype.

The following teacher's prompt from grade 10 explains that normal is a moving target:

> What is understood to be normal behaviour is neither fixed nor universal. It can vary from person to person and with time and place. What we think of as 'normal' behaviour and appropriate jobs and activities for males and females is very much influenced by our social and cultural backgrounds.
>
> Many of the assumptions that we make about normal behaviour can exclude people who identify as transmale, transfemale, or two-spirited, or who identify in other non-binary ways. People can have difficulty with family, peers, and others when they don't conform to these assumptions. They may be teased, isolated, threatened, or exposed to violence, and the resulting stress can affect their self-worth, sense of well-being, and overall health.[9]

I suppose there are some people who enjoy being eccentric or living "outside of the box" (I know a few!) but most of us want to belong, to be normal. And so, eliminating the hostility and finger-pointing that faces those who may be considered "abnormal" is a good goal.

Can we agree that the bullying, violence, and rejection faced by these youth is simply not okay while disagreeing that the approach taken by the curriculum is helpful? The fact is, this teacher prompt is a jumble of truth and trouble. It states rightly that people who don't conform to general assumptions about how gender is expressed *may* identify as **transmale, transfemale,** or **two-spirited**. It is also very true that these individuals may have relationship and social difficulties. As we discussed earlier, these difficulties can sometimes lead to a myriad of mental health issues including self-harm and suicide.

While my heart aches for these kids, I sadly cannot say that labeling this type of self-identification as normal will ultimately help them. It reminds me of the story of the Emperor's New Clothes. No matter how much you want to believe something is true, saying that it is doesn't make it so. The Emperor was told he was wearing new robes. He was actually naked. Transgenderism is not normal and pretending that it is will not change that. Doing so will ultimately cause more harm than good.

The teacher's prompt above stretches normal behaviour to include being born one gender yet in some or all ways, presenting as the other gender. What the prompt does not do is clarify that there are some people who do not conform to expected gender stereotypes, yet are still attracted to the opposite sex and/or identify 100% with their biological gender. Non-conformity doesn't equate to being LGBT. When the curriculum fails to acknowledge this very real, very normal possibility, confusion is likely to increase and false assumptions may be made, (e.g., that someone who is straight is gay and so on). It is clear from this prompt that teachers are expected to focus more on the slight chance that one of his or her students is transgender (0.3-0.6%[10]) than to teach that variation and diversity within each biological gender is expected and normal.[a]

---

[a] Such as in the Masculinity and Femininity Spectrums which are discussed in chapter 4.

Strategies for Challenging Stereotypes

Probably the most effective way to change stereotypes is to introduce and regularly expose students to less familiar elements that they may not see otherwise. The more students are exposed to something, the more normal and accepted it becomes.

The Canadian Teachers' Federation published a manual in 2012 entitled *Supporting Transgender and Transsexual Students in K-12 Schools* which states:

> The more educators work to break down sex role stereotypes ... the more inclusive their classrooms will become for all students who are questioning their gender and exploring facets of their identity. Breaking down stereotypes and releasing students from their gender straightjackets is one critical way in which educators can open up space for all students who define themselves as outside of the mainstream."[11]

So how is this accomplished in the classroom? I have identified four key strategies: read-aloud stories, strategic lessons, changing common terms, and desensitizing through exposure.

King and King
by Linda De Haan and Stern Nijland

In this stereotype-shattering fairy tale, a prince is told that it is time to wed. Several princesses visit the castle but the prince chooses the brother of one of the princesses to marry.

Read-Aloud Stories

Expanding a child's idea about what is normal begins in the early primary years. An obvious, effective way to do so is through carefully selected read-aloud stories. Interestingly, the grade 6 curriculum explicitly points this out: "We can understand people's sexual orientations better, for example, by reading books that describe various types of families and relationships. Not everyone has a mother and a father – someone might have two mothers or two fathers ..."[12]

While there are many children's books available which introduce a diverse range of families, sexual orientations, and gender identities, a few examples are highlighted throughout this chapter. Various organizations compile comprehensive lists of these books.[b]

Strategic Lessons

There are many other methods used to challenge children's attitudes and understanding of gender roles and expectations. The Gay, Lesbian & Straight Education Network (GLSEN) provides lessons and strategies to educators that support this goal. One such resource is called *Ready, Set, Respect* in which they advise teachers to:

> Make sure the analogies you use when teaching don't rely on ... a hetero-normative viewpoint ... one that expresses heterosexuality as a given instead of being one of many possibilities. Such a viewpoint can translate into the development of all kinds of images that reinforce the view. The assumption ... that a boy will grow up and marry a woman is based on such a viewpoint. [13]

In a lesson supplied by GLSEN, students in kindergarten to grade 2 draw pictures of known characters and dress them in different colours and styles of clothing than they would normally choose. Some examples are: "Cinderella in a knight's armor, Spiderman wearing a magic tiara, Bob the Builder with a cape, Angelina Ballerina playing football, etc."[14] Changing key elements of beloved characters whose behaviour and dress aligns so closely to traditional

---

[b] The "Rainbow Book List" highlights new "GLBTQ Books for Children and Teens" and is released every January. See http://glbtrt.ala.org/rainbowbooks/rainbow-books-lists

gender stereotypes is an obvious – and effective – way to challenge and break the stereotype. If Spiderman can wear a tiara, why not other boys?

Changing Common Terms

Ontario outsources the development of its health and physical education lessons to a not-for-profit organization called OPHEA – the Ontario Physical and Health Education Association. In 2014-2015, OPHEA's resources and communications were accessed by all of Ontario's 5,000 schools, 72 school boards, and 36 public health units,[15] making it by far the most influential and pervasive voice for instruction on health related topics and activities in the province. Lessons developed by this organization directly support the province's curriculum and are designed to be a comprehensive fit such that additional resources would not be required – the entire program can be delivered using the materials developed by OPHEA.

Here's what OPHEA has to say about the language of gender: "The language of 'boys' and 'girls' is gender interpreted, and it is more accurate to talk about anatomy rather than gender and use 'bodies with' or 'people with' language when referring to developments and changes in puberty."[16]

Here's how this plays out. Although teachers may choose to introduce this language earlier – for example in grade 1 when learning about genitalia – the first reference in the OPHEA materials is grade

And Tango Makes Three
by Justin Richardson and Peter Parnell

Based on a true story, Roy and Silo cuddle and share a nest like the other penguin couples. When the others start hatching eggs, a zookeeper gives them an abandoned egg.

2 when talking about stages of development and their components. When discussing infants, teachers would be encouraged to say, "People with vaginas grow to about half their adult height by 1½ years of age. People with penises grow to about half their adult height by 2 years of age." For a child age 2-10 years, "People with penises tend to be slightly taller and heavier than people with vaginas."[17] The section about adolescents uses "people with ..." terminology seven times. [18] Grade 4 material has student resources entitled, "Changes During Puberty for People with Penises/Vaginas," with drawings illustrating body changes for the two "types" of people. It's such a brain scratcher, I found myself thinking how awkward all the "people with" lingo became as I went through the material. *If only we had specific words we could use for people with penises or people with vaginas?*

If it wasn't so scary, it would be laughable how our society has become so divorced from common sense.

The Barrier of Media

To our discredit, children are already regularly exposed to heterosexual sexuality in the media (and more and more other forms of sexual expression as well) including television, the internet, and other sources. In order to eliminate the stereotype, if that is the goal, children are being intentionally exposed to the other options. A read-aloud story with fictional characters is one thing; seeing these scenarios acted out in the media by real people is another thing entirely.

Desensitizing through Exposure

While it is true that the average teacher will go to OPHEA for their health and physical education lesson material, there are other well-respected resources available as well. Depending on the mindset of the teacher in the room, these may be used heavily, moderately, or not at all, as teachers are given a lot of latitude for professional judgment.

As indicated in chapter one, the Toronto District School Board (TDSB) compiled a resource called *Challenging Homophobia and Heterosexism*[c] to address "inequities" in the curriculum. Its goal is to enable "all lesbian, gay, bi-sexual, trans-gendered, two-spirited, and queer (LGBTQ) students, and students who identify themselves on the basis of sexual orientation and gender identity, to see themselves reflected in the curriculum."[19] This wording is mirrored in the health curriculum.[20] The strategies in the TDSB resource have become a benchmark on addressing these issues.

There are several reasons for concern with the methods suggested by this resource. For starters, concepts and terminology are introduced which could damage children's innocence. In several instances, children are expected to brainstorm and/or are presented with sample names they might be called if they don't conform to gender stereotypes. In a kindergarten to grade 3 lesson, the following examples are given: "sissy, fag, gaylord, batty man, poof-

10,000 Dresses
by Robert Ewert

Every night, Bailey dreams about dresses but no one wants to hear about these dreams. "You're a BOY!" his parents say. "You shouldn't be thinking about dresses." Then Bailey meets Laurel, an older girl who is inspired by Bailey's courage.

---

[c] This resource was published two years after the 2010 Ontario sexual health curriculum was rejected and shelved, and contains much of the content which caused offense and parental outrage in both 2010 and 2015.

ta, tomboy, lezzy, lezbo, dyke, homo, queer, etc."[21] As a reasonably well-informed woman who works daily with children ages 4-12, I was not even aware of all of these terms! In a grade 4-6 lesson, the list expands with more terms such as, "Mama's boy, gay, weak, butch."[22] What benefit is perceived to be in supplying these labels to such young children? I take great issue with these derogatory words being openly introduced – even in guided context – within the walls of a classroom. How introducing these slanderous terms to young children is thought to be an effective way to reduce discrimination and bullying is beyond me.

It goes on. A grades 4 to 6 literacy lesson on "Gender and Relationship" exposes children to a range of visuals and content, particularly to do with same-sex relationships. Students challenge ideas of what is considered normal and desirable with the purpose of normalizing same-sex relationships. They confront their assumptions by asking "What is 'normal?' Why do you think that? Where do we get ideas of what is normal?"[23] Remember, according to the grade 6 curriculum, assumptions are "usually untrue."[24]

While examining this lesson, I became mortified. In the activities, children are to explore magazines that range from pop culture/mainstream to gay and lesbian, seeking images that break traditional and stereotypical expectations. By looking through the recommended resources, it was clear to me that students who do so are most definitely going to be exposed to graphic and highly suggestive images and content.

The lesson specifies that "if magazines are not available, this media activity can be done using TV images and/or the Internet as an alternative."[25] In today's classroom, with the technology that is readily available, this is a convenient option. With the demands on a teacher's time, there is a high possibility that a teacher may not preview each of the websites, trusting the individuals who created the lesson to have done so and deemed them appropriate. This means that even a teacher with the best of intentions may inadvertently use the lesson with their students, not realizing the danger.

Unbuckling the "Gender Straightjacket"

And danger there is.

I went onto these magazines' websites, something I do not advise because of the explicit material, to see what a 9 to 11-year-old child might encounter when browsing for this in-class activity. Here is just a sample of the content on these websites.

Magazine Resources in "Gender and Relationships" Lesson

Out Magazine "A gay and lesbian perspective on style, entertainment, fashion, the arts, politics, culture, and the world at large"
- Articles: "Meet the Hot Cop Who Went to Twerk at Pride Parade;" "Daniel Radcliffe Named Butt of the Year"
- Watch: "Pink Moon" (photo: two men in bed, sexual positioning); "Future Same-Sex Anthem: Hayley Kikoyo's 'Girls Like Girls'"
- Art and Books: "Meet Ren Huang: An Avid Chronicler of Erections & Other Earthly Delights"
- Popnography: "The Inevitable 'Magic Mike XXL' Porn Parody We've All Been Waiting For;" "Miley Cyrus gets Handsy with Stella Maxwell in Public" (photo: passionate kissing)[26]

Xtra Magazine A gay internet magazine, formerly in print
- Advertisements: "Hot 'n Horny Hookups: Non-Stop Hot Guys" with photos (links to "our other site"); other advertisements with blatant sexual innuendo
- Sex tab: "How I (almost) had sex with a woman: A bisexual foursome, a female orgasm, and pushing my limits;" "When your trick doesn't pay up;" "When your client wants to take drugs during sex;" "The joys of park sex"[27]

Curve Magazine "The nation's best-selling lesbian magazine"
- Articles: "My girlfriend won't have sex with me – what should I do?" "5 Great Lesbian Movies available on Netflix Streaming"[28]

I was blown away by the blatant, "in-your-face," sexual content on these websites that children may use as in-class resources! But when you consider the goal of the curriculum – sexual freedom – it makes sense, doesn't it? Desensitization is a very effective strategy, used time and again throughout history to normalize something that naturally offends. By viewing this kind of content in class, especially on a repeated basis, shock value is reduced, and the depictions are increasingly understood to be normal.

Lessons begin by examining what is considered normal for each gender and end with the expectation that previous norms will have less of a hold on the students involved. Along the way, students may be exposed to language, images, and suggestions that may damage not only their identity but their purity.

I can only assume that the writers of this lesson material were unaware of the pro-prostitution slant of the *Xtra* publication. Its crossover into this type of content is indicative of the moving line of morality.

The guiding principle in many Christian homes is, "Be careful little eyes what you see, little ears what you hear, and little feet where you go." It's become necessary to admit that when children's feet take them into a public school classroom where they are learning about gender stereotypes, their eyes may see images, and their ears may hear words that will not easily be forgotten. The result may even be that they come to form a false conclusion of whether they should see themselves as male or female or how they understand romantic relationships between men and women.

---

[1] Milton Diamond and H. Keith Sigmundson, "Sex Reassignment at Birth: A Long Term Review and Clinical Implications," *Archives of Pediatrics and Adolescent Medicine*, No 151 (March 1997), http://www.hawaii.edu/PCSS/biblio/articles/1961to1999/1997-sex-reassignment.html; John Colapinto, "The True Story of John / Joan," *Rolling Stone*, December 11, 1997, http://www.healthyplace.com/gender/inside-intersexuality/the-true-story-of-john-joan/.
[2] The Associated Press, "David Reimer, 38, Subject of the John/Joan Case," *The New York Times*, May 12, 2004, http://www.nytimes.com/2004/05/12/us/david-reimer-38-subject-of-the-john-joan-case.html?_r=1.

[3] Gayle Rubin, "The Traffic in Women: Notes on the 'Political Economy' of Sex," in *Toward an Anthropology of Women*, ed. R. Reiter (New York: Monthly Review Press, 1975) as quoted in Mari Mikkola, "Feminist Perspectives on Sex and Gender" (Stanford, CA: Stanford Encyclopedia of Philosophy, 2016) https://plato.stanford.edu/entries/feminism-gender/#GenSocCon.

[4] Kristopher Wells, Gayle Roberts, and Carol Allan, *Supporting Transgender and Transsexual Students in K-12 Schools: A Guide for Educators* (Ottawa: Canadian Teachers' Federation, 2012), 14, http://gendercreativekids.ca/wp-content/uploads/2013/10/Supporting-Transgender-and-Transsexual-Students-web.pdf.

[5] Ontario, Ministry of Education, *The Ontario Curriculum, Grades 1-8: Health and Physical Education*, 238.

[6] Kristen Berry, "Gender Differences in Teenagers," *Our Everyday Life*, 2017, http://oureverydaylife.com/gender-differences-teenagers-16388.html.

[7] Ontario, Ministry of Education, *The Ontario Curriculum, Grades 1-8: Health and Physical Education*, 177.

[8] Ibid.

[9] Ibid., 165.

[10] Gary J. Gates, "How Many People Are Lesbian, Gay, Bisexual, and Transgender?" (Los Angeles: The Williams Institute, April 2011), 5, http://williamsinstitute.law.ucla.edu/wp-content/uploads/Gates-How-Many-People-LGBT-Apr-2011.pdf; Andrew R. Flores et al., "How Many Adults Identify as Transgender in the United States?" (Los Angeles: The Williams Institute, June 2016), 2, http://williamsinstitute.law.ucla.edu/wp-content/uploads/How-Many-Adults-Identify-as-Transgender-in-the-United-States.pdf.

[11] Wells, Roberts, and Allan, *Supporting Transgender and Transsexual Students*, 14.

[12] Ontario, Ministry of Education, *The Ontario Curriculum, Grades 1-8: Health and Physical Education*, 177.

[13] Robert A. McGarry et al., *Ready, Set, Respect! GLSEN's Elementary School Toolkit* (New Tork: GLSEN, 2016), 4, https://www.glsen.org/sites/default/files/GLSEN%20Ready%20Set%20Respect%202016.pdf.

[14] Ibid., 43.

[15] "About Us," *OPHEA.net*, accessed January 26, 2017, https://www.ophea.net/about-us.

[16] "Identifying Sexually Transmitted Infections, Grade 7: Understanding Sexual Health and Decision Making," in *H&PE Curriculum Resources: Grades 1-8*, (Toronto: OPHEA, 2016), page 5 in lesson 4.

[17] "Body Changes, Grade 2: Understanding the stages of development," in *H&PE Curriculum Resources: Grades 1-8*, (Toronto: OPHEA, 2016), page 6 in lesson 1.

[18] Ibid., 7.

[19] Ast et al., *Challenging Homophobia and Heterosexism*, 2.

[20] Ontario, Ministry of Education, *The Ontario Curriculum, Grades 1-8: Health and Physical Education*, 67.

[21] Ast et al., *Challenging Homophobia and Heterosexism.*, 43.

[22] Ibid., 84.

[23] Ibid., 69.

[26] Ontario, Ministry of Education, *The Ontario Curriculum, Grades 1-8: Health and Physical Education*, 177.
[25] Ast et al., *Challenging Homophobia and Heterosexism*, 69.
[26] *Out Magazine - Gay & Lesbian Travel, Fashion & Culture,* accessed July 5, 2015 and January 26, 2017, http://www.out.com/.
[27] *Daily Xtra | Gay & Lesbian News,* accessed July 5, 2015 and January 26, 2017, http://www.dailyxtra.com/.
[28] *Curve Magazine - North America's Best-Selling Lesbian Magazine,* accessed July 5, 2015, http://www.curvemag.com/.

Picture books highlighted in this chapter:
Linda DeHaan and Stern Nijland, *King and King* (Berkley, CA: Tricycle Press, 2002).
Justin Richardson and Peter Parnell, *And Tango Makes Three* (New York: Simon & Schuster Children's Publishing, 2005).
Robert Ewert, *10,000 Dresses* (New York: Triangle Square, 2008).

Chapter 8

LOVE WHO YOU WANT TO LOVE

"Haven't you read', Jesus replied, 'that at the beginning the Creator made them male and female,' and said, 'For this reason a man will leave his father and mother and be united to his wife, and the two will become one flesh'?"

Matthew 19:4-6

After the 2011 census results were published, the headlines were dominated by reports that the number of same-sex married couples had increased by 42%.[1] This supposed "swell" of same-sex marriage analyzed data from the five-year period after same-sex marriage was legalized in Canada.

When we examine this data more closely, the 42% increase took this group from just 0.6% to 0.8% of all couples in Canada. In spite of what the headlines would lead us to believe, Canada is still an overwhelmingly heterosexual society.

The Changing Family

We live in an increasingly diverse culture and that includes our families. There is no longer one solid definition of what makes a family and it is the adults, not the children, who determine what form the family will take.

In my adult life, I have been in several different family situations. Married, divorced, a single mom, and remarried; my husband and I are raising my sons from my first marriage alongside our daughter. Statistics Canada calls this a "complex blended home" and for us, this is life. We have rebuilt and we have grown, but the reality of a family that has been broken is generally just below the surface.

Each family type has different strengths and struggles. I can also attest to some of them as a teacher, having had students and parent volunteers from immigrant families, one-parent, blended, and intact families, and families with children going through separation and divorce. Although I have not yet had a child from a same-sex home in my class, that day may come. Countless times I have taken a moment to chat with a child who is having a rough day, only to find out that the child is struggling to cope with something difficult or heartbreaking at home. For better or for worse, children bring their family lives into the school.

We have to acknowledge that children's families matter. The Ontario Ministry of Education has recognized this by including a strand in the grade 2 social studies program called "Changing Family and Community Traditions" in which students learn about different types of families. Those listed in the social studies curriculum are: "families with one parent, two parents, no children; same-sex families; blended and multigenerational families; immigrant families; [and] families where the parents come from different religious or ethnocultural groups)."[2] As I was analyzing this list, I began to wonder why the curriculum authors chose the examples they did and why they omitted others.

The table below highlights some of the family structures reported in 2011 by Statistics Canada.

Canadian Family Structure[3]

Families with no children	44.5%
Families with children under age 24 at home, living with two parents:	
Opposite-sex couple parents	99.84%
Same-sex couple parents	0.16%
Families with children under age 14 at home, by parent(s)' marital status:	
Married parents	67.0%
Common-law parents	16.7%
Intact families (children live with both parents) 87.4%	
Blended (step-families) 12.6%	
Single parent	16.3%
Families with children under age 14 at home, other factors:	
Multi-generational families	4.8%
Parents from different religious/ethnocultural groups	*not found*
Immigrant families	*not found*
With other relatives or non-relatives *	0.8%
With grandparents and not parents *	0.5%
In foster families *	0.5%
* family types not mentioned in the curriculum	

Keeping in mind that the examples in the curriculum are suggestions and not intended to be comprehensive, the Ministry *did* have to select examples. Along with some interesting inclusions, there are also glaring omissions, for example, children living in foster families (0.5%). Certainly, foster children form a group requiring acknowledgement and sensitivity. Among other concerns, this oversight underscores the fact that it is not sensitivity towards children that is driving this element of the curriculum but ideology.

The Ongoing Value of an Intact Family

It appears that the typical Canadian family with children is still opposite-sex (99.84%) and intact (children live with both parents, 87.4%). Studies and statistics have consistently shown that there are huge benefits to children when they are raised in stable, intact, two-parent families. The Canadian research body, The Institute of Marriage and Family Canada,[a] published a report entitled "Sticking With It," which aims to encourage parents "in non-abusive, low-conflict but troubled marriages" to persevere because of the clear value to kids. The report states:

- Children in single-parent homes are more likely to experience emotional distress, anxiety, and hyperactivity than children from two-parent homes.[4]

- Children with cohabiting biological parents were more likely to display hyperactivity and lack of impulse control than those with married biological parents.[5]

- Children from married, biological families were more likely to pursue post-secondary education than their peers from cohabiting and stepfamilies.[6]

Figuring out how children with same-sex parents are going to turn out will be answered over time with more research, however, I did find one Canadian study worth considering. This study from 2013 compared same-sex families to married, opposite-sex families and used high school graduation rates as a marker of success. The data showed that "children of married opposite-sex families have a high graduation rate compared to the others; children of lesbian families have a very low graduation rate compared to the others;

---

[a] Now CARDUS Family.

and the other four types [common law, gay, single mother, single father] are similar to each other and lie in between the married/lesbian extremes."[7]

It also found that "the particular gender mix of a same-sex household has a dramatic difference in the association with child graduation;" boys had lower graduation rates in lesbian households, while girls had lower rates in gay households.[8] This seems to challenge the assertion that mother and father roles are interchangeable. The author of the study even conceded that "there is the belief that mothers and fathers provide different parenting inputs that are not perfectly substitutable. These results would be consistent with this notion."

In changing the definition of marriage to include same-sex couples the definition of family was also changed. Sadly, this happened without giving much thought to the impact on children.

Having acknowledged that children bring their family lives to school with them, I would be remiss if I said that same-sex families should never be talked about at school – especially when there are children for whom this is the reality. In order for these children to feel accepted and safe, they need to sense that they are recognized and valued. This can't happen if typical family types are mentioned in the learning environment and the others are excluded.

The question is: can these children only be supported by promoting, normalizing and even celebrating diverse family structures?

Molly's Family
by Nancy Garden

When Molly draws a picture of her family, a kindergarten classmate insists that no one has two mommies. Her teacher and her two mothers help her accept her family.

The Barrier of Homophobia

The Elementary Teachers' Federation of Ontario (ETFO) has weighed in on this dialogue, recommending the following ways to link family diversity to the curriculum and therefore reduce homophobia:

> Make connections to the curriculum so all students feel validated and engaged.
>
> - Use LGBT books, media, and pictures as part of your everyday curriculum.
> - Include the terms gay, lesbian, bisexual, transgender when describing various families.
> - Use teachable moments to address homophobia or transphobia.[9]

How might these suggestions look in the daily classroom? To find the answer to this question, I went back to the Toronto District School Board resource, *Challenging Homophobia and Heterosexism*.

This resource includes a kindergarten to grade 3 lesson entitled "What Makes a Family." This lesson was designed to meet learning expectations in language, including writing, media literacy, and oral communication; the arts; social studies; and health. In the planning notes, teachers are instructed to familiarize students with key terms including *gay* and *lesbian* "to address the biases and stereotypes that may be associated with them."[10]

This lesson includes a read-aloud of "Who's in a Family?" by Robert Skutch, which includes examples of interracial, single-parent, grandparent-headed, and gay/lesbian families. Skutch discussed the book in a 2005 radio interview saying,

> The whole purpose of the book was to get the subject [of same-sex parent households] out into the minds and the awareness of chil-

dren before they are old enough to have been convinced that there's another way of looking at life ... It would be really nice if children were not subjected to the – I don't want to use the word 'bigotry,' but that's what I want to say anyway – of their parents and older people.[11]

Following the reading of the story, students participate in a drama activity about a variety of family types, role playing the opposite gender with boys playing girl roles and vice versa. Children are cautioned to avoid portraying images or behaviours of "stereotypical" families. They then create collages and pictures depicting a variety of family structures.

We have already established that there may be times when a discussion on same-sex families is necessary to accommodate for a child who lives in that setting. I would not argue against this, as that dialogue would be important in eliminating bullying and assisting the child. A carefully chosen read-aloud story *could* assist in that scenario as well.

However, that is not the situation in which this lesson is presented. This lesson (and others like it) are designed not so that students can see themselves and their families "reflected in the curriculum,"[12] but to encourage children to believe that you can love who you want to love, and that all forms of sexuality (and the resulting family structures) are morally equal. This is something that we have already established is contrary to God's will and design for families and children.

Who's in a Family?
by Robert Skutch

This children's book asks the question, "Is there a typical family?"

Addressing Diverse Family Structures at Home

The enemy is hard at work destroying the family and mutilating God's plan. The marriage relationship reflects the relationship of Christ to the church! How important that we keep God's model and plan alive, and make absolutely sure our children understand what God intended when He created marriage and the family.

As parents, we don't get to choose how the topic of "family" is handled in the classroom; we only get to address it at home. Therefore, we need to get it right.

Sin's Effect on God's Plan for Family

As discussed in the previous chapter, certain stereotypes are unnecessary and harmful. However, when we are talking about marriage as being between a man and a woman, we are not talking about stereotypes but the order that God set out in the very beginning for men, women, and relationships. If we allow our culture to replace God's design for marriage and go along with the idea that it's okay to "love who you want to love," then we lose something that God designed for our good. We settle for something that is not only the opposite of God's intention for his creation but is specifically harmful to the people involved, including the children.

God has a plan for each person. His plan is good. His plan is best. His plan is not that people would live unfulfilled lives as a "shell" of themselves because they are forced to sacrifice their sexuality. His plan is for abundance, fulfillment, and purpose but we need to trust him.

Jesus said, "The thief comes only to steal and kill and destroy; I have come that they may have life, and have it to the full."[b] Whoever suggests that you can come to God but hold onto your sin, is a thief who wants to steal God's best away from you. No matter who

---

[b] John 10:10

you are or what your struggle is with sin or temptation, surrendering to God's plan for your life is going to require sacrifice.

There's a meme I've seen that says, "Don't judge me because I sin differently than you do." I agree. We are not often in a place to judge although we may find ourselves in a position where we need to speak. And when we do, we need to be sure to speak the truth in love out of a desire to see God's plan for joy and fulfillment thrive in our culture and the lives of those around us.

So what is God's plan for marriage? We see it in God's creation of Adam and Eve, and his design of one man and one woman for life. Seeing Adam in the Garden of Eden God said, "It is not good for the man to be alone"[c] and he created a woman. He then directed the new couple to "be fruitful and multiply" – the first command to humankind. It's obvious that this command can only be followed fully and naturally through the sexual union of a man and a woman.

This poster is one of many similarly-themed posters on display in Ontario's public schools. Source: unlearn.com

After sin entered the picture, it affected everything including marriage. Sin has impacted the family dramatically through adultery, divorce, and same-sex relationships. Many children are raised in homes where there is no belief in God at all. This has changed the family unit and left kids hurting and broken.

---

[c] Genesis 1:28

When you talk about God's design for family with your child, you will find yourself talking about people who are in non-traditional family situations. Maybe your own family, like mine, has experienced some of these realities. When you lay a foundation with your children by teaching God's best plan for marriage, spend time talking about God's grace, forgiveness, and redemption too.

What About the Kids?

The focus upon same-sex families in the curriculum clearly supports the culture's desire to move "beyond tolerance to acceptance and respect" regarding all elements of diversity, in particular, the LGBT community. But what is the impact on the children?

In acknowledging family diversity in our culture, we need to recognize that some situations are just broken. This is tough for children as they try to deal with their home situation and the pressure that can be put on them to appear okay even though things may be hard or confusing. We should not shove this reality under the carpet to avoid social taboos.

As a parent, when you talk to your child, try to focus their attention on their peers rather than the adults. When tough questions arise, be careful not to divulge any more information than your child needs to know. Remind your child of the golden rule of treating others the way we would like to be treated. We need to teach our children to honour their classmates' dignity and value by not putting them down because of their family situation or for any other reason.

It should also be clear to our children that they should not judge others. Children can be taught to understand the principles we discussed in chapter one for how to lovingly handle this type of situation. Only God knows any person's whole story and why people make certain choices. We should never lead someone to believe that we think we are better than them. While our ultimate desire is for their healing and acceptance of God's best plan for their lives, being kind and loving is the best course of action because that was Jesus' example when He lived among sinners.

---

[1] "Swell of Same-Sex Families Ushering in 'the New Normal'," *CBC News, Montreal*, November 9, 2012, http://www.cbc.ca/news/canada/montreal/swell-of-same-sex-families-ushering-in-the-new-normal-1.1204886.

[2] Ontario, Ministry of Education, The Ontario Curriculum | Social Studies, Grades 1 to 6; History and Geography, Grades 7 and 8, 78.

[3] Statistics Canada, "Portrait of Families and Living Arrangements in Canada," *Statistics Canada*, accessed September 22, 2015, last modified December 22, 2015, http://www12.statcan.ca/census-recensement/2011/as-sa/98-312-x/98-312-x2011001-eng.cfm#a4.

[4] B. Ram and F. Hou, "Changes in Family Structure and Child Outcomes: Roles of Economic and Familial Resources," *Policy Studies Journal* 31, no. 3 (2003): 317–19, as quoted in Peter Jon Mitchell, "Marriage: How Sticking with It Can Pay off" (Ottawa: Institute of Marriage and Family Canada, August 12, 2015, http://www.imfcanada.org/archive/1094/marriage-how-sticking-it-can-pay.

[5] J. Gosselin et al., "Canadian Portrait of Changes in Family Structure and Pre-School Children's Behavioral Outcomes. Vol. 38:6, p. 523," *International Journal of Behavioral Development*, 2014, 38, no. 6 (2014): 523, , as quoted in Mitchell, "Marriage: Sticking with It."

[6] Ibid.

[7] Douglas W. Allen, "High School Graduation Rates among Children of Same-sex Households," *Review of Economics of the Household*, 11, no. 4 (2013):635-658, http://www.sfu.ca/~allen/REHAllen.pdf, brackets mine.

[8] Ibid.

[9] "Welcoming and Supporting Lesbian, Gay, Bisexual., and Transgender Families" (Elementary Teachers' Federation of Ontario), accessed June 17, 2015, http://www.etfo.ca/Resources/LGBTfamilies/Documents/SupportingLGBTFamilies%20.pdf.

[10] Ast et al., *Challenging Homophobia and Heterosexism*, 34-39.

[11] Robert Skutch, interview, *Here and Now,* National Public Radio, May 3, 2005, as quoted in "'Who's in a Family?' - in the Diversity Book Bag," *Mass Resistance*, accessed January 26, 2017, http://www.massresistance.org/docs/parker/diversity_book.html, brackets mine.

[12] Ibid.

Picture book highlighted in this chapter:

Nancy Garden and Sharon Wooding, Molly's Family (New York: Farrar, Straus and Giroux, 2004).
Robert Skutch, *Who's In a Family?* (Berkley, CA: Tricycle Press, 1997).

Chapter 9

Tossing Out the Trash

"Start children off on the way they should go, and even when they are old, they will not turn from it."

Proverbs 22:6

"Schools should stick to teaching reading, writing, and arithmetic!" As parents, we say and hear this but did you know that this has never been the true purpose of public schools? In the early days of education, the main intent was to teach children to read (most importantly the Bible) with hopes of creating healthy, productive communities where citizens could read and write laws by which they were to abide.[1] Laws were based on God's Word. So although the outward goal was to learn to read and write, the real function was to prepare students to be good citizens.

Good Schools Produce Good Citizens

In Canada's early days, schooling took place informally at home, preparing children for their livelihood and upcoming responsibilities as adults. Over time, as education became the role of the government, things began to change.

It might surprise you that the motivation of mass schooling was to "instill appropriate modes of thought and behaviour into children."[2] The Canadian Encyclopedia informs us that many parents believed in the value of public schooling because of the benefits of academic training.[3] I think most parents today feel the same way. However, early school promoters placed emphasis on "character formation, the shaping of values, the inculcation of political and social attitudes, and proper behaviour."[4] This approach hasn't changed either and has paved the way for some of the issues we have with public schools today. Since our culture has, for the most part, lost its common moral compass, who determines what are "appropriate modes of thought and behaviour?" Who defines what makes a good citizen?

The curriculum states that "parents are the primary educators of their children with respect to learning about values, appropriate behaviour, and ethnocultural, spiritual, and personal beliefs and traditions, and they are their children's first role models."[5] This seems like a good start to making a good citizen and it's important to know that this is contained in the curriculum. This underscores that a parent's judgment counts when it comes to what is good and appropriate for their own children. I encourage you to keep this in mind and refer to it when your rights and responsibilities as parents are questioned.

In reality however, there are contradictions in the curriculum about the role parents play in teaching their children about sexuality and gender roles. It begins as a "soft" mention in grade 5, where students consider "emotional and interpersonal stresses related to puberty" and the example of "conflicts between personal desires and cultural teachings and practices."[6] In grade 6, students discuss sources of support. The list begins with some promise because of examples that include "elders, family members, community agencies, churches, mosques, synagogues, public health units, telephone help lines, [and] recreation facilities,"[7] but only elaborates on telephone help lines.[a]

So what is the role that public schools play in making good citizens? The Ontario Human Rights Commission says it is an important one: "Public schools are intended to be institutions that foster tolerance and respect for diversity."[8] The Ontario Ministry of Education also emphasizes valuing diversity as a key to "establishing a just, caring society,"[9] and to "becoming critically thoughtful and informed citizens."[10]

It seems that good citizens these days value diversity, particularly diverse sexual and gender identities. As you'll see in the discussion that follows, belief systems that don't accept this are considered everything from "unhealthy" to "erroneous."

The Barriers of Religion and Culture

So what happens when being a "good citizen" collides with the religious, cultural, or family values of a home? In the table below, the grade-by-grade progression of references to family, religious, or cultural values is laid out. While exploring the topics of gender identity, gender expression, and sexual orientation, students are led to question their family or religious values. Along with the questions raised by the curriculum, a cursory overview of what the Bible has to say on these topics is provided.

---

[a] Later in this chapter is a discussion about the types of help lines that have been suggested.

The Curriculum on Family, Religious, or Cultural Values

Legend:
GI (Gender Identity)
SO (Sexual Orientation)

GRADE 7:[14]	GRADE 8:[13]	GRADE 9:[12]	GRADE 10:[11]
Decision: About sexual health	**Decision**: About sexual activity	**Decision**: How you feel about your GI or SO	**Decision**: How to respond to cultural misconceptions about sexuality and gender
Factors: GI, SO, cultural teaching	**Factors**: Awareness / acceptance of your GI & SO can be affected by cultural information, religious beliefs, media	**Factors**: Self-awareness, culture, religion, media, acceptance, stigma, stereotypes, homophobia, self-image	**Factors**: Understanding about GI and SO can be based on erroneous information
Prompts: Think about religious beliefs or moral considerations; decide to have sex or wait	**Prompts**: How people of all identities can develop a positive self-concept	**Prompts**: How culture, family background, religion, and values affect your sense of self	**Prompts**: Everyone has the right to live free from discrimination; some beliefs are based on erroneous information and lead to discrimination

BIBLICAL FACTORS FOR THESE DECISIONS

Sexual decision-making: "Flee from sexual immorality" (1 Cor. 6:18); "Honour God with your bodies" (1 Cor. 6:20); "Among you there must not be even a hint of sexual immorality" (Eph. 5:3); Sex is reserved for marriage between a man and a woman (1 Cor. 7:1-7; Matt. 10:8; Gen. 2:24)

How you feel about yourself: You were created for a purpose (Eph. 2:10); God has known and chosen you since before time began (Jer. 1:5; Eph. 1:4-5); God loves you with an everlasting love (Jer. 31:3); You are precious to God (Matthew 9:29-31); Your body is a temple of the Holy Spirit (1 Cor. 6:19-20).

How to respond to what you are taught at school: Test everything. Hold onto the good. Reject evil. (1 Thess. 5:20-21); Examine the Scriptures to see if what is being taught lines up with God's Word (Acts 17:11)

With this biblical foundation, children will be better prepared to handle the topic when it is addressed at school. If you aren't already convinced that this type of conversation is in your child's best interests, consider the potential impact of the following lesson from OPHEA, where grade 8 students discuss scenarios supplied by a fictitious blog:

> I'm in Grade 8. What do I do when my parents/guardians say "No way" to having a romantic/dating relationship? — Feeling Controlled
>
> I'm in a relationship that is getting serious. I am confused about sex and I am afraid I might lose my girlfriend. How can I keep my relationship with my girlfriend without having sex? — Too Close
>
> I'm pretty scared about dating and being pressured to do things I'm not ready for. What should I do? — Scared
>
> Many of my friends are interested in the opposite sex, but I am not. I'm confused. What should I do? — Questioning[15]

There is no doubt these questions are thought provoking and have the potential to initiate in-depth conversation with kids who are considering sexual activity. However, for the Christian family, there is risk in having a child consider personal limits and make a plan about sexual activity in an environment that may not uphold faith or family values. "Parents say no to dating?" What could a teacher or peers say about that? "Dating relationship getting serious?" What does *serious* look like at the age of thirteen?

Evaluating Cultural and Religious Messages

Although the Ministry of Education funds the development of health lessons for elementary grades through OPHEA, it does not provide similar resources for its high school curriculum. In these scenarios, teachers look for resources or ideas from their board or community partners. I found a lesson endorsed by Planned Parenthood on the topic of cultural misconceptions about sexuality and gender. Because of this organization's direct contributions to and support of the curriculum this would be considered a partner with valuable resources for the classroom.[b][16]

This lesson's goal is for students to learn that "some messages from their culture can support them in being healthy and ... other messages can promote unhealthy behaviors."[17] To get the conversation started, students bring home a questionnaire about "My Culture." They survey family members to identify cultural messages about health, sex, and gender. Some sample responses listed are:

- Couples should wait until they are married to have sex.
- People shouldn't talk about sex.
- It is okay to be gay or lesbian.
- Boys should play sports, but girls should focus on working around the house.
- Both girls and boys should go to college.
- It is okay for women to be ministers and men to be nurses.[18]

After sorting the messages into "positive" and "negative" lists, a discussion is held. The following advice is given: "Focus ... on the positive messages. Acknowledge that our cultures help make up who we are. Fortunately, we have received some very positive messages about our health, sexuality, and gender from our cultures. These can be viewed as strengths we receive from our culture." "Tell youth that, unfortunately, not all the messages they generated are

---

[b] "Planned Parenthood Toronto strongly endorses the implementation of the updated curriculum. Youth need and deserve accurate information about sexual health that goes beyond pregnancy and disease. The updated curriculum addresses many issues, including consent, in age appropriate ways that will enable youth to make informed choices. We congratulate the Ministry, and thank them for doing the right thing." - Sarah Hobbs, executive director, Planned Parenthood Toronto.

positive or healthy (note the major assumption that "negative" messages will be received from home). Ask the group: what can you do when you receive negative and unhealthy messages from your culture that you do not believe or do not want to accept?"[19]

- Ask parents ... about the message. Maybe there is more to the message OR a positive message that you did not notice.
- Investigate what other peoples' cultures teach them about the issue.
- Choose not to accept the message as part of your life.
- Look to other elements of your culture for more healthy messages.
- Connect with role models and mentors who support your healthy behaviors.[20]

As Christians, we should be aware that the Bible, which we believe to be the inspired Word of God, has a great deal to say about sexuality. Furthermore, God – as the author of creation – gets the final word on gender. Therefore, as we have already explored in chapters three and four, there can be no gray area when it comes to sex and gender. What the lesson describes as negative messages or unhealthy behaviours may actually be referring to firmly-held religious beliefs based on God's Word, such as those listed in the table earlier in this chapter.

For example, a child may bring to the lesson the belief that "I should wait until I am married to have sex" or that "homosexual practices go against God's Word and are wrong." Would this child be pressured not to "accept this message as a part of their life?"[21] I believe that is a possibility. In this lesson, students are guided into sorting through their religious belief systems, and tossing out whatever doesn't coincide with the curriculum. Who would have thought that Christian values and ideals would be considered trash?

This lesson takes instruction of religious and cultural values *away* from the family and puts it *into* the hands of the teacher delivering the lesson. This violates the principle of the curriculum itself, which says that parents are the primary educators of our children when it comes to values, behaviours, and belief systems.[22]

Evaluating My Own Identity

In the table, "The Curriculum on Family, Religious, or Cultural Values," you can see that the topic of "erroneous beliefs" and "misconceptions" about sexuality are a focus in grade 10. These are just fancy words for *wrong beliefs about sexuality.* Let's head to the curriculum to see exactly how this is presented.

> Describe some common *misconceptions about sexuality* in our culture, and explain how these may cause harm to people and how they can be responded to critically and fairly.
>
> *Teacher prompt:* Understanding about gender, gender identification, and sexual orientation varies widely and can be based on *erroneous* information.[23]

Because the schools perceive a lack of support in certain homes due to "misconceptions" or "erroneous beliefs," children who are questioning their sexuality or identity are encouraged to seek support elsewhere. The curriculum lists supports for students who need help understanding and accepting their gender identity and sexual orientation. Some of the examples in grade 8 include role models (people of similar ages or cultures), family support, school support (trusted adults), support through community partners, and Gay-Straight Alliances.[24] Let's look into what is meant by a few of the supports mentioned in this list.

School Support

Every school has a variety of staff to help a student in need. Teachers are at the top of this list. The curriculum affirms that "teachers often find themselves in the role of caring adult for students. This can be a fulfilling and also challenging responsibility, particularly when students choose to disclose personal information."[25] Students will sometimes divulge problems, abuse, or struggles to a trusted teacher, who then needs to know what to do with the information. This is a very important part of the teacher-student relationship. Ideally, the teacher is a trustworthy adult who is available to help a child through difficulties. It is usually a relationship that works in the best interests of the child, especially when the parents and teacher work together.

However, when the home and school have different ideas about what is best, there are circumstances when the school holds the ultimate power over a decision. In particular, if the home is deemed "homophobic," the school is *legally allowed* to exclude parents from certain decisions and information in its attempt to form the child into a good citizen. You will remember this is because of the authority given to them by Policy Memorandum 145.

Without parental knowledge, schools can refer students to "board resources or to a community-based service provider that can provide the appropriate type of confidential support ... (e.g., counselling; a sexual assault centre; Kids Help Phone; Lesbian, Gay, Bisexual, Transgendered [LGBT] Youth Line."[26] Similarly, board employees "are expected to support students – including those who disclose or report incidents and those who wish to discuss issues of healthy relationships, gender identity, and sexuality – by providing them with contact information about professional supports."[27]

Community-Based Service Provider

Who are "community-based service providers"? It's an important question to ask. They could be counsellors, including those at sexual health clinics. They might work at a sexual assault centre, or they may be a "help line" such as the Kids Help Phone or the LGBT Youth Line. In order to figure out what kind of support might be offered, I went on the LGBT Youth Line website, innocently addressed as *www.youthline.ca*. I expected to find a variety of resources for youth who struggle with mental health or social issues related to their sexual orientation or gender identity. While they do operate a phone and online chat service, their website primarily consists of links to other organizations. There are some resources listed under the Links and Resources page that may provide mental, emotional and social support for LGBT youth seeking help.

The Referral Database is another story.

Most "community partners" have partners of their own. Acting as "a friend of a friend," the community partner may introduce children to their other partners either directly (through a referral), or indirectly (through their website). Referrals on the LGBT Youth Line database include but are not limited to, the following categories of support.

- Parents
- Needle exchange
- Social Club
- Bisexual
- Gender Identity
- Abuse
- Bar/Nightclub
- Bath House
- Christian
- Church

- Coming Out
- Crisis Line
- Distress
- Drop-In
- Family Planning
- Harm Reduction
- Lending Library
- Peer Mentoring
- Pride
- Sexual Violence

- Spa
- STD
- Suicide
- Support Group
- Text Support
- Women
- Workshops
- Worship
- Youth Program[28]

WARNING! The following section contains descriptions of websites directly linked from the LGBT Youth Line. Some information is sexually suggestive and graphic. Every effort has been made to balance the truth about what is supplied with the need to encourage purity of thought. Please use discretion and ultimately, I do not recommend you seek out these websites.

Referrals from the LGBT Youth Line include links to:

- A bathhouse in Toronto which describes itself as a "private men's gym, sauna, bathhouse for men 18 years and older you know, men looking for other men!" The website is explicit that this is a place for males to explore their sexual fantasies with one or many partners. It advertises, "Students free for 90 days!"

- A bisexual networking group that holds support meetings on a monthly basis. The meetings involve discussion on topics brought up by those in attendance, followed by "informal social time at a nearby restaurant or bar."

- A nightclub website advertising events with the following titles (no descriptions provided): "Kink 101, Jock Strap, Pup Night," (Pup night?) "Trade, Naked Night, Sin" and so on.

Friends, these are just the first three I clicked on, on the first page! There were many, many more but I chose to stop because I felt I had seen enough to establish significant concerns. In fact, my concern was such that I reported the LGBT Youth Line Referrals page to Cybertip and called a police officer friend from my church congregation. The police officer assured me that he shared my concern but the reality is that this is a hotline that deals with sexuality and what is provided is going to be sexual in nature. I pressed him, certain that some law is being stretched or broken in supplying these types of introductions to *children*. He assured me that there likely isn't.

The role of schools and their community partners, in my opinion, is to ensure the safety of the children in their care and under their influence, not to encourage dangerous or erotic sexual exploration. Not surprisingly then, I did not hear back from Cybertip.

Gay-Straight Alliance

Among the list of supports for students who are questioning their gender identity and sexual orientation is the Gay-Straight Alliance

(GSA). A GSA is a school club run by students with one or two teachers who serve as advisors. It is described as:

> A safe place for any and all students to meet and learn about all different orientations, to support each other while working together to end homophobia, and to raise awareness and promote equality for all human beings. In addition to being a group dedicated to support, it also strives to educate the surrounding areas and the community on different gender and equality issues. [29]

Members of a GSA are "lesbian, gay, bisexual, trans, two-spirited, queer, and questioning (LGBTQ)," along with heterosexual members and members with LGBT family or friends (also called "allies").[30] Students may have conversations about topics related to LGBT issues, and organize events or awareness campaigns. A GSA must legally be formed in any school where there is a student who is willing to take the lead.[31]

Who is Your Child's Go-To?

When teachers provide support that is affirming of LGBT identities or students are referred to GSAs or community partners, there's little doubt that the intent is to "help." However, this is where the importance of a common worldview is critical. What will these people speak into that child's life? If a child is experiencing same-sex attraction (or wonders if they are) they may hear that nothing can or should be done other than accepting a gay identity.

So who *can* your child talk to if they have a question about their identity or sexuality? Parents, it's you! You need to be in the game. Granted, there are going to be times when your child does not feel comfortable talking to you. What then? Make sure your child is aware of some safe, go-to supports when they have those tough questions.

The fact is that when a child is feeling vulnerable, the person who speaks into their lives has a tremendous amount of influence. It is our hope as parents that the person who answers their questions shares our family's values. It is natural that parents want to have a voice. But if not you, then your child needs to be aware of other options: people who know the truth about who they are in Christ and will remind your child when they need to hear it. As a teen, I would seek out my youth pastor or an older mentor as I worked through issues. Their listening ears and wise counsel directed me back to God and His plan for me. Who can your child turn to?

Raising children means so much more than just producing good citizens, although it is our hope that our children will love their country and respect its laws. As Christian parents, we trust, we pray, and we strive to have children who grow up to honour not just their country but their Lord.

---

[1] "On This Day ... Massachusetts Passes First Education Law," *Mass Moments*, 2017, http://www.massmoments.org/moment.cfm?mid=113.
[2] Chad Gaffield, "History of Education - The Canadian Encyclopedia," *Historica Canada*, March 4, 2015, http://www.thecanadianencyclopedia.ca/en/article/history-of-education/.
[3] Ibid.
[4] Ibid.
[5] Ontario, Ministry of Education, *The Ontario Curriculum, Grades 1-8: Health and Physical Education,* 13.
[6] Ibid., 158.
[7] Ibid., 172.
[8] Zwibel, "Faith in the Public School System
[9] Ontario, Ministry of Education, Realizing the Promise of Diversity, 10.
[10] Ontario, Ministry of Education, *The Ontario Curriculum | Social Studies, Grades 1 to 6; History and Geography, Grades 7 and 8,* 6.
[11] Ontario, Ministry of Education, *The Ontario Curriculum, Grades 9-12: Health and Physical Education*, 124.
[12] Ibid., 104.

[13] Ontario, Ministry of Education, *The Ontario Curriculum, Grades 1-8: Health and Physical Education,* 215-6.

[14] Ibid., 195-6.

[15] "Understanding Healthy Development | Making Informed Decisions about Sexual Health, Grade 8| Dear Grade 8," in *H&PE Curriculum Resources: Grades 1-8,* (Toronto: OPHEA, 2015), lesson 2.

[16] Ontario, Ministry of Education, "Support for the Updated Health and Physical Education Curriculum," *Ontario Newsroom,* February 23, 2015, https://news.ontario.ca/edu/en/2015/02/support-for-the-updated-health-and-physical-education-curriculum.html.

[17] "Learning Activities: The Culture Connection," *ReCAPP: Resource Center for Adolescent Pregnancy Prevention,* 2017, http://recapp.etr.org/recapp/index.cfm?fuseaction=pages.LearningActivitiesDetail&pageID=160&PageTypeID=11.

[18] Ibid.

[19] Ibid.

[20] Ibid.

[21] Ibid.

[22] Ontario, Ministry of Education, *The Ontario Curriculum, Grades 9-12: Health and Physical Education,* 13.

[23] Ibid., 126 (emphasis mine).

[24] Ontario, Ministry of Education, *The Ontario Curriculum, Grades 1-8: Health and Physical Education,* 216.

[25] Ontario, Ministry of Education, *The Ontario Curriculum, Grades 9-12: Health and Physical Education,* 15.

[26] Ontario, Ministry of Education, "Policy/Program Memorandum No. 145," 10.

[27] Ibid., 5.

[28] "Referral Database," *LGBT Youth Line,* accessed August 24, 2015, http://www.youthline.ca/get-support/referral-database/.

[29] "My GSA," *Egale: Canada Human Rights Trust,* 2015, http://egale.ca/portfolio/mygsa/.

[30] Ibid.

[31] Ibid.

Chapter 10

THE SILENCE IS DEAFENING

*"Then you will know the truth
and the truth will set you free."*

John 8:32

What do you do when the truth gets in the way of what you really want to do? Some people would change their goal. Others might hide the truth.

When it comes to sexual freedom, the truth is being treated like a dirty little secret. It has been compromised, glossed over, and pushed aside in order to encourage students to explore their sexuality, all the while under the impression that they are free from any real consequences.

The Barrier of Stigma

Welcome to Truth-Bending 101. Let's look at some of the ways the curriculum has bent the truth to reduce the stigma associated with HIV and homosexuality, as well as advance the notion of sexual freedom.

Truth-Bender #1: Condoms Protect Against HIV and STIs[1]

The elementary school curriculum says this about condom use:

> Use "condoms consistently if and when a person becomes sexually active" ... "Condoms help to protect you against STIs [Sexually Transmitted Infections], including HIV" ... "To prevent the transmission of HIV, avoid behaviours associated with greater risks of HIV transmission, like vaginal or anal intercourse without a condom and injection drug use. It is very important that you use a condom if you do have sex."[2]

The secondary school curriculum has this to say:

> Describe the relative effectiveness of various methods of preventing unintended pregnancy or sexually transmitted infections (STIs), including HIV/AIDS (e.g., avoiding oral, vaginal, and anal intercourse; delaying first sexual intercourse; using protection, including barrier and hormonal methods, to prevent unintended pregnancy; using condoms and dental dams to protect against STIs) ...
>
> *Student Response:* Using a condom every time is one of the most effective methods of birth control and will reduce your chances of getting an STI, including HIV.[3]

The OPHEA lesson for seventh grade continues to prop up the use of condoms but does acknowledge that a "small risk" exists even when a condom is used: "Engaging in sexual activities like oral sex, vaginal intercourse, and anal intercourse without protection means that you can be infected with an STI. Even with the use of a condom or dental dam, there is still a small risk."[4]

Truth

The fact is that very few people use condoms "perfectly," that is, consistently (every time) and correctly (with no breakage or leakage). Even when used "perfectly," condoms are only about 85% effective in preventing HIV.[5] Statistically speaking that means one out of six sexual encounters with an HIV infected person will result in infection regardless of condom use. Or put another way, "for every 100 cases of HIV infection ... about 15 (range: 7 to 24) would happen when condoms are used consistently."[6]

HIV and **AIDS** are ongoing epidemics in the 15-29 age group, with nearly one-quarter to half of all new cases arising in this demographic.[a][7] Almost 10,000 people between the age of 13 and 24 in the United States were diagnosed with HIV in 2013.[8] Between 1985 and 2014, 26% of all HIV cases in Canada were among youth.[9] Our youth deserves the truth so they do not become victims of this devastating disease. As the U.S. Food and Drug Administration states:

> Condom use cannot provide absolute protection against any STD. The most reliable ways to avoid transmission of STDs are to abstain from sexual activity or to be in a long-term mutually monogamous relationship with an uninfected partner. However, many infected persons may be unaware of their infection because STDs often are asymptomatic and unrecognized. In other words, sex with condoms isn't totally "safe sex," but it is "less risky" sex.[10]

---

[a] This, and many of our statistics, come from CATIE – Canadian AIDS Treatment Information Exchange. CATIE obtains the majority of their data and their funding from the governmental Public Health Agency of Canada. See more at http://www.catie.ca/.

Clearly, if you are having sex, you should be using a condom. It is correct to say that your chances of getting an STI including HIV are *reduced* when you use a condom but they are not *eliminated*.

The type of information about condoms that has been included in the curriculum has been shown to lead to increased sexual risk behaviour and often higher – not lower – HIV infection rates.[11] It gives youth a false sense of security about the true risks of having sex. Teens and preteens generally feel invincible and this extends to their sexuality. This makes them more likely to have unprotected sex. Downplaying the risks of HIV infection only adds to the likelihood of this irresponsible behaviour.

HIV is not the only risk. Another study that only examined for chlamydia, gonorrhea, or trichomonas showed that in "sexually active African-American teen girls, despite 100 percent condom use, one in five became infected ... within twenty-eight months."[12]

Condoms do not work well as protection against STIs that are spread through skin-to-skin contact. These include HPV (which can cause cancer),[b] genital herpes, and syphilis (a life-threatening disease).[13] This is because some infected areas are not covered by the condom (e. g. the scrotum, vulva, and surrounding areas). Furthermore, it has been shown that individuals infected with an STI are at an increased risk of becoming infected with HIV.[14]

Far from being the solution to STIs and HIV, condoms provide a false sense of security to teens. It is irresponsible to not provide all the facts so that teens and preteens can make truly informed decisions about risky behaviour, properly slotting "safer sex" into that category.

---

[b] Although not all types of HPV (Human papillomavirus) lead to cancer, HPV is the main cause of cervical, anal, and esophageal cancer. Of over 100 types of HPV with varying degrees of impact to your health, the HPV vaccine only protects against four and is ineffective against 30% of the cancers.

Truth-Bender #2: Anal Sex is No Riskier than Other Forms of Sex

Anal sex is not treated separately from other sexual behaviours, being consistently included in the curriculum with oral sex and vaginal intercourse.[15] This leads to the assumption that it is no different – including no riskier – than other forms of sex.

This faulty notion is supported by Canada's highest government. In the lead-up to the July 2016 Toronto Pride Parade, Prime Minister Justin Trudeau indicated that his government was looking to move on lowering the age of consent for anal sex (currently at age 18) to match the age of consent for vaginal sex (currently at age 16).[16]

> "Condoms provide some protection, but anal intercourse is simply too dangerous to practice."
>
> C. Everett Koop,
> former US Surgeon General

Truth

Anal sex is estimated to be 17-20 times riskier than vaginal for HIV infection.[17] Former Surgeon General C. Everett Koop warns, "Condoms provide some protection, but anal intercourse is simply too dangerous to practice."[c][18]

In spite of this, teen girls do not see anal sex as particularly risky. In fact, one study showed that 41% of urban minority females have

---

[c] Everett Koop was US Surgeon General from 1982-1989, yet current medical advice still recognizes the increased risk of HIV with anal sex (see endnote 36). This quote originally appeared on the FDA website but in 2014 it was removed with no explanation, apparently after it was quoted by a US government official opposed to the implementation of comprehensive sex education in Hawaii. Source: http://www.hawaiireporter.com/food-and-drug-administration-alters-condom-warning-on-its-website-without-citing-any-reason.

anal sex as a means of birth control and 20% thought that HIV could not be transmitted through anal sex.[19] A 2016 study analyzed by Dr. Frederick Gandolfo, gastroenterologist,[d] revealed that 37% of women and 5% of men have had anal sex, with women having the most anal sex in their twenties and the numbers dropping off from there.[20]

Neither the elementary nor the secondary school curriculum provide us with any hope of getting the true facts into the minds of teens. In these curriculum documents, vaginal and anal intercourse are consistently listed side by side, presented as equal behaviours. Children are simply told that it is risky to have *vaginal or anal intercourse* without a condom. The substantial, added risks of anal sex are not elaborated upon. Being unaware of the increased risks, many teen girls see anal sex as a preferred alternative to vaginal sex in order to avoid pregnancy.

Let's compare the suitability of the vagina and the anus for receiving sexual intercourse.

- Both the vagina and the anus have a lining that creates a barrier which keeps viruses as far as possible from the bloodstream. Other STIs can damage the barrier and sex can create microscopic tears which increase the risk of viral transmission.[21] The lining of the vagina is 20-45 cells thick.[22] The lining of the anus is one cell thick.[23]

- Unlike the anus, the vagina is naturally lubricated for the purpose of sexual intercourse. Without this natural lubrication, there is increased friction and stresses during anal intercourse. This leads to a couple of risks:
    - Condoms are more likely to break.

---

[d] A gastroenterologist is a medical doctor specializing in the digestive system (the esophagus, stomach, small intestine and large intestine (colon), gallbladder, pancreas and liver).

- The delicate one-cell-thick lining of the anus is very easily torn by the friction, giving infections quick and easy access to the bloodstream. This allows for potential HIV infection *within ten minutes* of having anal sex with an infected partner![e] [24]

If that isn't enough, let's look at other serious risks that are compounded by anal sex. A study cited by the CDC showed that 60 percent of *HIV-negative* gay and bisexual men have HPV.[25] Being HIV-positive further increases the risk for anal cancer.[26] The CDC also states that men who have sex with men have a *17 times* greater risk of developing anal cancer than heterosexual men.[27] We can assume that the risk for anal cancer is also increased for women who have anal sex, particularly if they are already infected with HPV.

HPV is transmitted during vaginal sex and is commonly connected to an increased risk for cervical cancer. The lesser known fact is that HPV can also be transmitted during anal sex and about 95% of anal cancers are caused by HPV.[28] People who have receptive anal intercourse are at increased risk for HPV infection of the anus, anal dysplasia, and anal cancer.[29]

Another rather "icky" fact that is unmentioned in the curriculum: anal sex can lead to fecal incontinence (stool leaking from the anus). The 2016 study mentioned earlier confirms this.

> The internal anal sphincter muscle is responsible for ... keeping the anus closed, and keeping stool inside where it belongs ... Anal sex may simply dilate and stretch the anal sphincter muscle and eventually cause damage to the muscles themselves, and/or cause sensory nerve damage leading to loss of sphincter sensation and control.[30]

---

[e] This has been observed in vitro (tissues in a lab) but not in vivo (in actual sexual contact).

This has been said before – clearly, the anus is designed to be an exit, not an entrance.

Finally, anal sex brings the risk of coming into contact with feces (this is often downplayed as a "minimal" risk). Feces are filled with "salmonella, shigella, amoeba, hepatitis A, B, and C, giardia, campylobacter, and others. These organisms and others can be transmitted during anal sex or during oral-anal contact"[31] and this contact can lead to serious health implications.

With the risks involved in anal sex, our youth need to be informed of the danger. As Dr. Gandolfo's analysis of the 2016 study concluded, "You probably just shouldn't do it."[32]

Truth-Bender #3: HIV is a Manageable Illness

The curriculum takes a serious look at HIV in grade 7, addressing some of the concerns around an HIV diagnosis. It states that HIV "is a serious viral infection that can be controlled with treatments." It attacks the body's immune system but "with treatment, the damage that HIV does … can be slowed or prevented." The curriculum is clear that HIV cannot be cured but goes on to say that "when people get tested for HIV early in the infection and access HIV treatments, they have the opportunity to live a near-to-normal lifespan." Further, "HIV can be transmitted whether or not someone has symptoms of the infection. However, HIV treatment can reduce the amount of HIV in someone's body to the point where it is much less likely that HIV will be transmitted."[33]

Have you noticed a trend? For every true statement about this life-altering, fatal disease, a dubious "bright side" is shared.

What advice does the curriculum give to those who wish to avoid exposure to HIV? "Avoid behaviours associated with greater risks of HIV transmission, like vaginal or anal intercourse without a condom and injection drug use. It is very important that you use a condom if you do have sex."[34]

Truth

Dr. Nadine Nyhus, a medical doctor and psychiatrist in Cambridge, Ontario, says the curriculum skipped over certain critical facts about HIV. She says that teens have the right to know what the curriculum isn't saying about an HIV infection. We've already established that even with "perfect" condom use, there is an increased risk of STI transmission, so what else does the curriculum overlook that is a cause for a concern?

Dr. Nyhus also wants teens to be aware that if they get infected with HIV, they may have to adopt children; they will not be able to breastfeed; and their ability to live in other countries will be restricted. Her conclusion is that "the curriculum significantly minimizes the reality of HIV infection. This kind of vaguely optimistic information is perhaps part of the reason for some evidence that condom use is down and the HIV infection rate is rising again among teens."[35] The table, "What You Should Know About HIV," highlights some of her key points of concern.

We pointed out earlier that anal sex carries a significantly higher risk of transmitting HIV when compared to vaginal sex. However, it is worth noting that heterosexual women are at higher risk of contracting HIV than heterosexual men.[36] This risk is even higher for young girls as a teen girl's immature cervix is not prepared to withstand infection. Nyhus is particularly concerned that the curriculum fails to adequately address the increased risk of HIV and STI infection for teen girls. In the teen years, the cervix is covered with a single layer of tissue that is very vulnerable to STIs.[f] As a girl ages into

---

[f] The tissue covering the cervix in the teen years is a completely different type of tissue than what covers the cervix in the 20's and beyond. The tissue in a teen's cervix is called columnar tissue. These cells have much greater height than width. Free Dictionary by Farlex | Medical Dictionary. Accessed February 11, 2017 at http://medical-dictionary.thefreedictionary.com/squamous+epithelium.

her 20s, the cervix matures and is replaced by thicker tissue[g] which is much more resistant to infection.[37]

What You Should Know About HIV

The curriculum says	The curriculum doesn't say
HIV "can be controlled. With treatment, the damage that HIV does to the body's immune system can be slowed or prevented. But HIV infection cannot be cured ... HIV treatment can reduce the amount of HIV in someone's body to the point where it is much less likely that HIV will be transmitted."[38]	If diagnosed with HIV, "you will have to take strong medications (two to four at a time) for the rest of your life ... Missed doses can result in treatment failure (viral resistant) so your life will be regimented. In addition, the medication can damage organs,"[39] and often leads to liver and kidney failure.
"HIV is transmitted through contact with bodily fluids ... To prevent the transmission of HIV, avoid ... vaginal or anal intercourse without a condom and injection drug use. It is very important that you use a condom..."[40]	If you have HIV, "you should never have intercourse without a condom for the rest of your life."[41]
"Today, when people get tested for HIV early in the infection and access HIV treatments, they have the opportunity to live a near-to-normal lifespan."[42]	Men who have sex with men (MSM) are 42 times more likely than the general population to die from HIV.[43] Life expectancy at age 20 for MSM is "8 to 20 years less than for all men ... nearly half of gay and bisexual men currently aged 20 years will not reach 65."[44]

The biology of a teen girl's body clearly points to the medical necessity to wait to have sex. As Dr. Grossman (mentioned previously in chapter six) says, this is not for "moral reasons, and not for emo-

---

[g] The tissue in a grown woman's cervix is known as squamous tissue. These cells are flattened and platelike (Ibid.). With many layers of squamous tissue, a woman's cervix is much more resistant to infections.

tional reasons (although these are significant as well) ... but for medical reasons alone."[h] [45]

In an effort to reduce stigma, the serious nature of an HIV diagnosis is downplayed by the curriculum and the culture at large, leading to lessened concern over exposure to HIV. Consequently, it is not surprising that the number of new HIV infections reported annually has not significantly decreased since the 1990s.[46]

Truth-Bender #4: Homosexual and Transgender Individuals are Not Connected to an Increased Risk for HIV

The curriculum makes no reference to the significantly increased risk of HIV infection associated with transgendered persons and men who have sex with men (MSM).

Truth

The reality is that transgendered, gay, and bisexual males or other MSM are at an extremely increased risk for HIV.

- According to the Public Health Agency of Canada (PHAC), in 2014 MSM accounted for 48.8% of all HIV infections and 63.3% of HIV infections in males.[47] The numbers are even higher in the United States with the Centre for Disease Control (CDC) reporting 67% of all HIV infections are in MSM.[48]

- MSM are 42 times more likely than the general population to die from AIDS.[49]

- Across Canadian cities, as many as 11-23% of MSM are living with HIV[50] and in addition, there are an estimated 18% of MSM who are unaware of their HIV-positive status[51] and

---

[h] For parents who want to access more information about this topic, I recommend Dr. Miriam Grossman's book, *You're Teaching my Child What? (Washington: Regnery Publishing, Inc., 2009).*

therefore wouldn't see the need to take additional precautions.

- Anal sex is the riskiest type of sex for getting or transmitting HIV with reports ranging from 17 to 20 times likely than vaginal sex and is how most MSM acquire the virus.[52]

Gay men are at increased risk for a variety of sexually transmitted diseases (STIs) like syphilis, gonorrhea, and chlamydia[53] as well as anal cancer[54] and viral hepatitis.[55] More new cases of AIDS surface among MSM than any other group.[56]

The health risks of women who have sex with women are not as dramatically different than those experienced by strictly heterosexual women. Some research shows that women who have sex with women have the same or higher rates of sexually transmitted infections.[57] There has also been some research which shows a higher prevalence of bacterial vaginosis, hepatitis C, and HIV risk behaviours in women who have sex with women.[58] And although this seems counter-intuitive, lesbian teens are reported to be twice as likely as their heterosexual peers to experience unintended pregnancy.[59]

Lesser known but equally concerning, are the increased rates of HIV among transgendered individuals in particular – second only to MSM.[60] A shocking 22-28% of transfemales in the United States are HIV-positive.[61] Likewise, Canadian researchers estimate 27.7% of transfemales live with HIV.[62] Female to male transgender have lower rates of HIV at 2-3%,[63] but there are emerging concerns. Women taking testosterone may be at greater risk for HIV because of changes that hormonal therapy make to the vaginal lining, but so far there have been limited studies to confirm this.[64]

Truth-Bender #5: Reducing Stigma is One of the Best Ways to Stop the Spread of HIV

The suggestion is made by the curriculum that "one of the best things you can do to stop HIV is to stop the stigma that is associated with having the infection."[65]

Read this statement very carefully: The curriculum says that stopping the stigma around HIV infection is the *best approach* for stopping HIV. I suppose the hope is that if there is no stigma, then people would be more likely to disclose their HIV-positive status before having sex with you. Based on what we've discussed above, does that sound like the best way to reduce the risk? What about the large number of people *who do not know* they are HIV-positive? What about the ongoing risk of infection even when all the precautions are taken?

One of the many collaborators of Ontario's new sex education curriculum was the Canadian AIDS Society. Part of this society's mission is to "promote a sex-positive perspective ... we encourage an open attitude toward sexuality and want people to talk about it, to embrace the joys it has to offer and to celebrate it, in all of its diverse forms."[66] The Canadian AIDS Society weighs in on stigma and discrimination against people with HIV, citing a study that 82% of Canadians living with HIV still have this experience. This, even though they state that "HIV is now considered a manageable disease."[67] It blames ongoing stigma on the following:

- Misunderstandings and inaccurate information about HIV and how it's transmitted
- Judgments made due to the fact that HIV is contracted through drug use and sexual activities, which are often highly stigmatized
- HIV's life-threatening nature[68]

Truth

It is unacceptable for individuals with HIV or AIDS to receive poorer quality health care or less support from their loved ones as a result of stigma. Nevertheless, it is (unfortunately) necessary that those who are considering having sex with an HIV-infected person recognize this to be a dangerous and even potentially lethal act. The risks are simply *too real* and *serious* for any other course of action. Attempting to eliminate the stigma of HIV by downplaying the risks is a gross act of negligence on part of the Ministry of Education.

I have spoken with some of my fellow teachers who say that they are aware of and teach some of the additional facts laid out in this chapter. I am thankful for these teachers. It's worth underlining that my statements in this chapter – in fact in the book as a whole – cannot speak to the practice in each individual classroom but to what the curriculum lays out to be covered.

In a stark contrast to the requirements of the curriculum, the law treats HIV as it would a weapon. Although it has been interpreted differently in various lower-court decisions, currently the law dictates that you must disclose your HIV-positive status before having sex.[69] In a recent example, one man who failed to disclose his HIV status was convicted of murder and even declared a dangerous offender when two of his sexual partners died as a result of exposure to HIV.[70] When the courts treat this disease so seriously, how can education ethically downplay its risks?

Just Say No!

Preparing students with the long list of facts we presented above means that they can be fully informed when considering sexual activity. As well, in order to truly shield our children, the concept of sexual abstinence should be given real consideration for its medical benefits alone. So how is abstinence handled in the curriculum?

We know abstinence is the only way to fully ensure non-sexual exposure to HIV, STIs and to negate other risks such as pregnancy. Yet the idea of not starting, stopping, or limiting behaviours medically proven to increase exposure to STIs is only mentioned as an ideal (e.g., delay sexual activity until teens are older).

In the curriculum, the term abstinence is vague and even misused. Although the curriculum's glossary uses the term in reference to "abstinence from all forms of sexual intercourse and other sexual activities,"[71] the teacher prompt in grade 7 handles the concept differently. This prompt suggests that abstinence "can mean different things to different people. People can also have different understandings of what is meant by having or not having sex. Be clear in your own mind about what you are comfortable or uncomfortable with."[72]

Although the definition itself is clear enough, the teacher prompt misses the mark! In what other area of health education do we encourage students to make up their own mind about what risks they are willing to assume? When handling poisons? When considering drug use? When making a decision whether or not to smoke? No, in these cases the curriculum is always clear and consistent: saying "no" and making health-minded decisions is the only acceptable answer to ensure optimal ongoing health. Why does the curriculum treat sexual activities with the accompanying high risks differently?

Following the logic of this teacher prompt, some people define abstinence as only referring to vaginal sex. Those who define it in that way are still at risk for STIs that are transmitted through oral or anal sex, even with condom use. If not having vaginal sex is someone's definition of abstinence, then they are primarily abstaining just from the activity associated with getting pregnant. They are not taking into consideration the serious medical risks associated with other sexual activities.

The underlying belief of the writers of the curriculum is that children having sex is more of a "when" than an "if." Starting sexual activity as an adult exclusively within a committed, monogamous relationship with an uninfected partner (in other words, true abstinence), is not even entertained as a possibility in the actual curriculum expectations.

Since the schools aren't teaching true abstinence, we must. Rick Hiemstra of the Evangelical Fellowship of Canada (EFC) suggests that as Christian families and churches we challenge this. He says we need to empower our children to reject the idea that saying "No!" to sex before marriage is impossible.

> One thing I've noticed about the curriculum is that it assumes that our kids are on their own and that they will constantly be negotiating sexual relationships with the people around them. The curriculum then tries to train them to be good negotiators. I haven't seen anyone question this and say, "Why should we abandon our kids to these endless rounds of negotiation?"
>
> In the Christian faith [sexual relationships] are circumscribed by marriage and marriage carries with it the responsibility to reflect the relationship between Christ and his church, and responsibilities to children, and responsibilities to wider family structures ...
>
> When we say "save sex for marriage" and that is supported by communities, it's a protection for kids from the need to negotiate sexual relationships. They can say, "This is wrong, and my family, my church and my community back me. So it is illegitimate for you to proposition me." It means that they have our support to refrain from opening negotiations.[73]

Our children need our support – both as families and as the church. Teens also need clear rules and protection during a stage of life where their sense of immortality may lead them to take risks that in later years they would reject or regret.

Let's talk like sane adults for a moment here and contrast the curriculum's approach to decision-making about sex with its treatment of decision-making about smoking. With smoking cigarettes, the curriculum clearly leads students to understand that saying "No" is the healthiest choice and that they are capable of doing so.[74] Students are repeatedly told that they can be – and need to be – strong against the pressure to begin smoking. Note the following examples.

Grade 1

"Smoking is bad for you and so is breathing smoke that is in the air when other people are smoking. We can ask people not to smoke around us."[75]

Grade 4

Students learn about nicotine and how addictions work. They learn about the health effects of smoking.[76] Students are given strategies such as "saying no strongly and clearly, giving reasons, changing the topic, making a joke, asking a question" in order to avoid pressure to smoke.[77]

Grade 5

"I can say strongly and clearly that I do not want to participate."[78]

Grade 6

"You have to … think about what you really want and what you value, and make up your own mind about things. Even if someone tells you 'everyone is doing it', your decisions are your own and so are the consequences."[79]

Imagine if our children were given the same type of empowering information we see above to help them deal with the pressure to have sex. In the past 15 years, Canadian provinces have seen a significant decrease in smoking among youth across the board.[80] We can only assume that the abstinence approach to smoking is working. If children were told the truth that sex outside of a monogamous, heterosexual relationship is high-risk and that we as adults believe they have the ability to say "No!" to sex before marriage, what would the impact on HIV and STI levels be?

The approach currently taken by health education curriculums across Canada and elsewhere is a clear move away from authentic education. Education is supposed to enable children to make informed decisions for healthy outcomes. Missing and misleading information does the opposite by keeping them ignorant of the facts.

---

[1] Ontario, Ministry of Education, *The Ontario Curriculum, Grades 1-8: Health and Physical Education,* 196-7.

[2] Ibid.

[3] Ontario, Ministry of Education, The Ontario Curriculum, Grades 9-12: Health and Physical Education, 103.

[4] "Identifying Sexually Transmitted Infections, Grade 7: Understanding Sexual Health and Decision Making" in *Curriculum Resources: Grades 1-8,* (Toronto: OPHEA, 2016), page 4 in lesson 4.

[5] "HIV & AIDS Information: Condoms and Lubricants - Do Condoms Work?," *NAM aidsmap,* 2017, http://www.aidsmap.com/Do-condoms-work/page/1746203/.

[6] Ibid.

[7] L. Challacombe, "The Epidemiology of HIV in Youth," *CATIE,* 2015, http://www.catie.ca/en/fact-sheets/epidemiology/epidemiology-hiv-youth; R. K. Thomas and D. Bartelli, "HIV Services for a New Generation," *Marketing Health Services* 21, no. 4 (January 2001): 24–29, as referenced in Miriam Grossman, *You're Teaching My Child What?* (Washington, D.C.: Regnery Publishing, Inc., 2009), 89.

[8] "Adolescent and School Health | Sexual Risk Behaviors: HIV, STD, & Teen Pregnancy Prevention," accessed January 27, 2017, https://www.cdc.gov/healthyyouth/sexualbehaviors/..

[9] Challacombe, "The Epidemiology of HIV in Youth."

[10] "Male Condoms and Sexually Transmitted Diseases," *U.S. Food & Drug Administration,* October 24, 2016, http://www.fda.gov/ForPatients/Illness/HIVAIDS/ucm126372.htm.

[11] "Comprehensive Sexuality Education (CSE): Sexual Rights vs. Sexual Health" (Family Watch International), accessed January 26, 2017, http://www.familywatchinternational.org/fwi/documents/fwipolicybriefCSE.pdf.

[12] R. A. Crosby et al., "Value of Consistent Condom Use: A Study of Sexually Transmitted Disease Prevention among African American Adolescent Females," *American Journal of*

Public Health 93, no. 6 (June 2003): 901–2, as referenced in Grossman, *You're Teaching My Child What?*, 89, available at https://www.ncbi.nlm.nih.gov/pmc/articles/PMC1447864/.

[13] "Condom Fact Sheet In Brief | Condom Effectiveness," *Centers for Disease Control and Prevention*, March 5, 2013, https://www.cdc.gov/condomeffectiveness/brief.html.

[14] James Wilton, "STIs: What Role Do They Play in HIV Transmission?," *CATIE - Canada's Source for HIV and Hepatitis C Information*, Spring 2012, http://www.catie.ca/en/pif/spring-2012/stis-what-role-do-they-play-hiv-transmission.;

[15] Ontario, Ministry of Education, *The Ontario Curriculum, Grades 1-8: Health and Physical Education*, 195-7; Ontario, Ministry of Education, *The Ontario Curriculum, Grades 9-12: Health and Physical Education*, 103.

[16] Steve Weatherbe, "Trudeau Promises to Decriminalize Anal Sex for 16-Year-Olds," *LifeSiteNews*, July 6, 2016, https://www.lifesitenews.com/news/trudeau-promises-to-decriminalize-anal-sex-for-16-year-olds.

[17] Pragna Patel et al., "Estimating per-Act HIV Transmission Risk: A Systematic Review," AIDS 28, no. 10 (June 2014): 1509–19, http://journals.lww.com/aidsonline/Fulltext/2014/06190/Estimating_per_act_HIV_transmission_risk___a.14.aspx; Grossman, *You're Teaching My Child What?*, 87.

[18] U.S. Food & Drug Administration, "Condoms and Sexually Transmitted Diseases," brochure, 1990, as quoted in Grossman, *You're Teaching My Child What?*, 91.

[19] B. O. Boekeloo and D. E. Howard, "Oral Sexual Experience among Young Adolescents Receiving General Health Examinations." *American Journal of Health Behaviour* 26, no. 4 (August 2002): 306–14.

[20] Frederick Gandolfo, "Does Anal Sex Cause Fecal Incontinence?," *Gastroenterology & Endoscopy News*, February 25, 2016, http://www.gastroendonews.com/Retroflexions/Article/03-15/Does-anal-sex-cause-fecal-incontinence-/35422.

[21] James Wilton, "From Exposure to Infection: The Biology of HIV Transmission," 2011, http://www.catie.ca/en/pif/fall-2011/exposure-infection-biology-hiv-transmission.

[22] Grossman, *You're Teaching My Child What?*, 97-100.

[23] Wilton, "From Exposure to Infection"; Clare Collins and Lisa Rossi, "Rectal Microbicides Fact Sheet," *Microbicide Trials Network*, August 11, 2016, http://www.mtnstopshiv.org/node/2864.

[24] J. P. Kraehenbuhl and M. R. Neutra, "Molecular and Cellular Basis of Immune Protection of Mucosal Surfaces," *Physiological Review* 72, no. 4 (October 1, 1992): 853–79, as referenced in Grossman, *You're Teaching My Child What?*, 99.

[25] "Tracking the Hidden Epidemics, Trends in STDs in the United States (2000)" (Centers for Disease Control and Prevention, 2000), https://www.cdc.gov/std/trends2000/trends2000.pdf.

[26] "Gay and Bisexual Men's Health: Sexually Transmitted Diseases," *Centers for Disease Control and Prevention*, March 9, 2016, https://www.cdc.gov/msmhealth/STD.htm.

[27] Ibid.

[28] "Human Papillomavirus (HPV) Vaccines," *National Cancer Institute*, November 2, 2016, https://www.cancer.gov/about-cancer/causes-prevention/risk/infectious-agents/hpv-vaccine-fact-sheet.

[29] Irving Salit and Rachelle Paquette, "HPV, Anal Dysplasia and Anal Cancer," *CATIE - Canada's Source for HIV and Hepatitis C Information*, 2016, http://www.catie.ca/en/factsheets/cancers/hpv-anal-dysplasia-and-anal-cancer.

[30] Gandolfo, "Does Anal Sex Cause Fecal Incontinence?"

[31] Presentation by Dr. Ruth Jacobs, as referenced in Grossman, *You're Teaching My Child What?*, 89.

[32] Gandolfo, "Does Anal Sex Cause Fecal Incontinence?"

[33] Ontario, Ministry of Education, *The Ontario Curriculum, Grades 1-8: Health and Physical Education,* 197.

[34] Ibid.

[35] Nadine Nyhus, "Opinion: Sex Ed Curriculum Inadequate and Should Be Withdrawn," Waterloo Region Record, July 8, 2015, http://www.therecord.com/opinion-story/5711922-opinion-sex-ed-curriculum-inadequate-and-should-be-withdrawn-doctor-says.

[36] Pragna Patel et al., "Estimating per-Act HIV Transmission Risk: A Systematic Review," *AIDS* 28, no. 10 (June 2014): 1509–19, http://journals.lww.com/aidsonline/Fulltext/2014/06190/Estimating_per_act_HIV_transmission_risk___a.14.aspx.

[37] Nadine Nyhus, email message to author, May 9, 2016.

[38] Ontario, Ministry of Education, The Ontario Curriculum, Grades 1-8: Health and Physical Education, 197.

[39] Nyhus, "Opinion: Sex Ed Curriculum."

[40] Ontario, Ministry of Education, *The Ontario Curriculum, Grades 1-8: Health and Physical Education,* 197, emphasis mine.

[41] Nyhus, "Opinion: Sex Ed Curriculum," emphasis mine.

[42] Ontario, Ministry of Education, *The Ontario Curriculum, Grades 1-8: Health and Physical Education,* 197.

[43] Travis Hottes, Ferlatte, and Gesink, "Suicide and HIV as Leading Causes of Death among Gay and Bisexual Men: A Comparison of Estimated Mortality and Published Research: Critical Public Health: Vol 25, No 5."; Travis Hottes, *Suicide is a Major Cause of Death for Gay and Bisexual Men*, April 9, 2014, http://cbrc.net/articles/09-2014/suicide-major-cause-death-gay-and-bisexual-men.

[44] R. Hogg et al., "Modelling the Impact of HIV Disease on Mortality in Gay and Bisexual Men," *International Journal of Epidemiology* 26, no. 3 (June 1, 1997): 657–61, doi:10.1093/ije/26.3.657.

[45] Grossman, *You're Teaching My Child What?*, 80.

[46] Public Health Agency of Canada, Centre for Communicable Diseases and Infection Control, "HIV/AIDS Epi Updates: National HIV Prevalence and Incidence Estimates for 2011," (Ottawa: Minister of Public Works and Government Services Canada, October 2014), http://www.phac-aspc.gc.ca/aids-sida/publication/epi/2010/1-eng.php#a0503.

[47] Public Health Agency of Canada, Centre for Communicable Diseases and Infection Control, "HIV and AIDS in Canada: Surveillance Report to December 31, 2014" (Ottawa: Minister of Public Works and Government Services Canada, November 2014), https://www.canada.ca/en/public-health/services/publications/diseases-

conditions/summary-estimates-hiv-incidence-prevalence-proportion-undiagnosed-canada-2014.html

[48] "HIV in the United States: At A Glance," last modified December 2, 2016, https://www.cdc.gov/hiv/statistics/overview/ataglance.html.

[49] Hottes, Ferlatte, and Gesink, "Suicide and HIV".

[50] L. Challacombe, "The Epidemiology of HIV in Gay Men and Other Men Who have Sex with Men," *CATIE*, 2017, http://www.catie.ca/fact-sheets/epidemiology/epidemiology-hiv-gay-men-and-other-men-who-have-sex-men.

[51] L. Challacombe, "The Epidemiology of HIV in Canada," CATIE, 2017, http://www.catie.ca/en/fact-sheets/epidemiology/epidemiology-hiv-canada.

[52] Liz Highleyman, "Just How Risky Is It? Studies Shed Light on HIV Risk and Prevention," *BetaBlog*, June 4, 2014, http://betablog.org/studies-shed-light-on-hiv-risk-and-prevention/; Patel et al., "Estimating per-Act HIV Transmission Risk."

[53] Centers for Disease Control and Prevention, "STDs in Men Who Have Sex with Men," *Centers for Disease Control and Prevention*, November 11, 2011, https://www.cdc.gov/std/stats10/msm.htm.

[54] CDC, "Sexually Transmitted Diseases," *Centers for Disease Control and Prevention*, March 9, 2016, https://www.cdc.gov/msmhealth/std.htm.

[55] CDC, "Viral Hepatitis," *Centers for Disease Control and Prevention*, February 29, 2016, https://www.cdc.gov/msmhealth/viral-hepatitis.htm.

[56] Duncan MacKellar et al., "Unrecognized HIV infection, Risk Behaviors, and Perceptions of Risk among Young Men Who Have Sex with Men: Opportunities for Advancing HIV Prevention in the Third Decade of HIV/AIDS," *Journal of Acquired Immune Deficiency Syndromes* 38 no.5 (2005): 324-5.

[57] Carmen Logie, "Queer Women are Ignored in HIV Research: This is a Problem and Here is Why it Matters," *CATIE Blog*, February 3, 2016, http://blog.catie.ca/2016/02/23/queer-women-are-ignored-in-hiv-research-this-is-a-problem-and-here-is-why-it-matters/

[58] K. Fethers, Caron Marks, Adrian Mindel, and Claudia S. Estcourt, "Sexually Transmitted Infections and Risk Behaviors in Women Who Have Sex with Women," *Sexually Transmitted Infections* 76 (2000): 345-49.

[59] "Lesbians and Birth Control," *Youth Resource,* accessed February 19, 2017, http://youthresource.com/health/women/index.htm

[60] National Center for HIV/AIDS, Viral Hepatitis, STD, and TB Prevention, *"CDC-Funded HIV Testing: United States, Puerto Rico, and the U.S. Virgin Islands, 2013* (Atlanta: Centers for Disease Control and Prevention, 2013), 28, https://www.cdc.gov/hiv/pdf/library/reports/cdc-hiv-CDCFunded_HIV_Testing_UnitedStates_Puerto_Rico_USVI_2013.pdf; CDC, "HIV Among Transgender People."

[61] Centers for Disease Control and Prevention, "HIV Among Transgender People," *Centers for Disease Control and Prevention*, April 2016, https://www.cdc.gov/hiv/pdf/group/gender/transgender/cdc-hiv-transgender.pdf.

[62] K. Beausoleil, and J. Halverson, Public Health Agency of Canada, presentation at *Towards the Development of a Coordinated National Research Agenda for Women, Transwomen, Girls and HIV/AIDS in Canada: A Multi-stakeholder Dialogue*, April 2011, as referenced in

Interagency Coalition on AIDS and Development, "HIV and Transgendered/Transsexual Communities," *ICAD-CISD,* August 2011, http://www.icad-cisd.com/pdf/HIV_and_Trans_Communities_EN.pdf

[63] Glenn Betteridge and Michael G. Wilson, Ontario HIV Treatment Network, "Transgender Men's Sexual Health and HIV Risk," *Rapid Review*, no 33 (September 2010:1), http://www.ohtn.on.ca/Pages/Knowledge-Exchange/Rapid-Responses/Documents/RR33-2010-TransMen-HIV.pdf;

[64] World Health Organization, *Policy Brief: Transgender People and HIV, WHO,* 2015, http://apps.who.int/iris/bitstream/10665/179517/1/WHO_HIV_2015.17_eng.pdf?ua=1&ua=1.

[65] Ontario, Ministry of Education, *The Ontario Curriculum, Grades 1-8: Health and Physical Education,* 197.

[66] "Sexual Activities." Canadian AIDS Society.

[67] "HIV, Stigma and Discrimination," *Canadian Aids Society,* accessed May 12, 2016, http://www.cdnaids.ca/files.nsf/pages/HIV-Stigma-and-discriminati/$file/CAS_WAD_InfoSheet_HIVStigma_EN.pdf.

[68] Ibid.

[69] E. Mykhalovskiy, Glen Betteridge, and D. McLay, "HIV Non-Disclosure and the Criminal Law: Establishing Policy Options for Ontario. Toronto. A Report Funded by a Grant from the Ontario HIV Treatment Network.," August 2010, http://www.catie.ca/pdf/Brochures/HIV-non-disclosure-criminal-law.pdf.

[70] Kimberley Gale, "HIV Killer Ruled Dangerous Offender," *CBC News, Canada*, August 2, 2011, http://www.cbc.ca/news/canada/hiv-killer-ruled-dangerous-offender-1.927621.

[71] Ontario, Ministry of Education, *The Ontario Curriculum, Grades 1-8: Health and Physical Education,* 227.

[72] Ibid., 196.

[73] Rick Hiemstra in email to the author. "Ontario Health Curriculum: Parent Resource," October 1, 2015.

[74] Based on a comparison made by Dr. Miriam Grossman, presentation regarding the OH&PE Curriculum in Mississauga, Ontario, August 18, 2015.

[75] Ontario, Ministry of Education, *The Ontario Curriculum, Grades 1-8: Health and Physical Education,* 95.

[76] Ibid., 141.

[77] Ibid., 143.

[78] Ibid., 158.

[79] Ibid., 174.

[80] Jessica Reid, David Hammond, and R. Burkhalter, "Tobacco Use in Canada: Patterns and Trends, 2015 Edition" (Propel Centre for Population Health Impact, University of Waterloo, 2015), http://tobaccoreport.ca/2015/TobaccoUseinCanada_2015.pdf.

Chapter 11

IT'S ALL ABOUT ME

*"For we are God's handiwork,
created in Christ Jesus to do good works,
which God prepared in advance for us to do."*

Ephesians 2:10

It was 1987 and I had just turned 14 (yes, go ahead ... do the math). It was the golden summer between grades 8 and 9 when I woke up to the realization that I had the freedom to form my own identity.

I was very aware of the waking-up process. I began to listen to radio stations of my own choosing, rather than albums approved by my parents. I sought independence by riding my bike everywhere and enjoyed the freedom that I discovered in the area of Hamilton, Ontario that locals call "the mountain." I made $5 an hour at my first summer job ironing shirts. This was more than a dollar above the $3.90 student minimum wage of the time – I was raking it in hand over fist! My friend Dianne and I, as savvy investors, spent a good chunk of that money on water guns, gag items at the dollar store, and Super Big Gulps at the 7-11.

Riding my bike as much as I was, I went from physically awkward to much more slim and athletic, and began to enjoy a new appreciation from my peers that stunned me. I had my first two boyfriends: the first I met at church in the youth group and the second at summer camp.

The summer was full of new experiences that shine brilliantly in my memory compared to the somewhat cloudy and indistinct memories that came before. Each moment of that summer has a sparkling quality, a fresh newness to it. I was becoming aware of myself and the world around me in a way I hadn't before.

It was in this summer that I chose to identify with Christ. I had prayed the salvation prayer as a three-year-old and was baptized when I was eight but until 1987 my faith remained that of a child. Growing up, I was learning about God, attending church clubs and Sunday School, and memorizing lots of Scripture verses. These activities prepared and grew me for the time when I would choose to become a follower of Jesus. At fourteen, my eyes were opened to what it means to identify as a Christian – to be a disciple of Christ – and I chose Jesus at camp under the leadership of my youth pastor. The years following reflected the fact that I made a life-changing decision in the summer of 1987.

Clearly, the age of fourteen was a very important year in my life. Maybe you remember a similar metamorphosis in your early teen years. As Char and I talked about this chapter and the topic of self-awareness, we recognized that the curriculum broaches this subject in grades 8 and 9 for a very specific purpose, one that resonates with our own experiences. While different people may take different paths or timelines to self-awareness, it's fair to say that the early teen years are critical periods of identity formation.

Those who developed the curriculum are clearly aware of the turning point many experience in their early teens. It's during these key years that students are presented with the concepts of self-image, self-awareness, and identification.

The Barriers of Self-Awareness and Self-Concept

The hoped- and worked-for outcome of the curriculum is full acceptance of LGBT identities, both by the culture and by the person who has taken on or is considering that identity. To achieve this, the Ontario curriculum seeks to remove all barriers that stand in the way of this goal.

We've examined several of these barriers in detail. We took a close look at **stereotypes**. We quickly saw that certain stereotypes which paint a large group with the same brush can be harmful and should not be promoted. However, we also uncovered an attack on the order God has set out for men, women, and relationships – things that are not stereotypes at all but natural responses to our God-given biological sex, stemming from God's design for the genders.

We looked at how various **media** including websites, magazines, and books are being used to desensitize children in order to reduce **homophobia**. We learned how picture books and cross-curricular lessons reinforce the new "normal," which is, of course, that there is no normal for family, gender, or relationships.

We saw what happens when being a "good citizen" collides with one's **religion** or **culture**: a child is encouraged to reject ideologies that oppose sexual freedom and regard LGBT identities as harmful and immoral. These ideologies are labelled misconceptions and erroneous.

And finally, we analyzed how the curriculum selectively handles the risks associated with sex, including HIV and STIs. We saw that the curriculum expects all types of sex to be seen as equally acceptable. We also saw that critical life- and decision-altering information is being withheld in order to promote the idea that you can have sex without serious consequences – all in the name of eliminating *stigma*.

As a student makes his way through public education, it is the hope of those who teach and support the type of comprehensive sex education typified by the Ontario curriculum that the barriers listed above will ultimately dissolve. At each stage, students are encouraged to be self-aware, to evaluate what they've been taught, and to come to know and accept themselves and their identity. If all goes as expected, children will have no difficulty accepting any and all gender identities and sexual orientations, both in others and in themselves.

Having cleared the hurdles of stereotypes, media, homophobia, religion, culture, family values and stigma, the final hurdles of self-image and self-awareness are all that's left. Children who have been taught for years that biological sex is insignificant in determining gender; that sexuality is meant to be explored instead of restrained; and that ideas that object to this are outdated and bigoted, now look inside themselves and make their own choices as shown in the table "The Journey of Self-Awareness."

Self-Awareness

Self-awareness begins in infancy when babies realize they are separate beings from their mothers. As children mature they begin to notice differences between themselves and others. They realize what they like and don't like; what they are good at and not-so-good at. Being aware of our needs and desires, and strengths and weaknesses is key to becoming well-balanced, mature adults. This self-awareness is a major contributor to forming our identity as we recognize the things, people, and ideas that resonate most with us. Undeniably, self-awareness is the catalyst that asks, "Who am I?" and "What do I identify with?"

The Journey of Self-Awareness

THE CURRICULUM TEACHES

➜ **Grade 1**: The differences in genitalia between boys and girls, (e.g., penis, testicles, vagina, vulva).[1]

➜ **Grade 3**: Visible and invisible differences in others make each person unique (e.g., "personal or cultural values and beliefs, gender identity, sexual orientation, family background").[2]

➜ **Grade 5**: Factors that cannot be controlled and form my identity include "whether I am male or female, my gender identity, sexual orientation … All of these things is a part of who I am. I cannot control these things, but I can control what I do and how I act."[3]

➜ **Grade 6**: My self-concept is affected by cultural and gender identity.[4] Body image and acceptance by others influence it too.[5]

➜ **Grade 8**: Decisions about sexual activity are affected by awareness and acceptance of gender identity and sexual orientation.[6] Individuals of all identities and orientations can develop a positive self-concept through acceptance by self, family, and community. A lack of support can be harmful.[7]

➜ **Grade 9**: Cultural/ family/religious background, media images, and acceptance or lack of acceptance by others, etc. can influence a person's understanding of their gender identity and sexual orientation. Assumptions about masculinity and femininity and "heterosexuality as the norm" can affect the self-image of those who do not conform, making it difficult to feel accepted.[8]

THE THOUGHT PROCESS

I need to understand the difference between *gender* and biological *sex*.

Gender and sexual identity are as integral to "Who I am" as culture and family background.

I evaluate my gender and sexual preferences and accept these things as an unchangeable part of my identity.

I AM SELF-AWARE

How others see me is a factor in my self-image and self-concept.

What is my gender identity? What is my sexual orientation?

I am developing a positive SELF-CONCEPT

Everyone needs to get on board with my gender identity and sexual orientation. Society needs to change.

I ACCEPT MY GENDER IDENTITY AND SEXUAL ORIENTATION AND OTHERS DO TOO.

As I shared at the beginning of the chapter, the early teen years are a critical time of identity forming. Teens begin to separate from their parents and are more focused on friends and extra-curriculars. During Charlotte's transition into the teen years, she went from being very interested in the army and war history in grade 6 and 7, to forsaking any aspirations to the military after a brief stint in the Air Cadets. About the same time, she sought to be unique from her peers by sporting a pixie cut while other girls competed to see whose bangs could be the puffiest. Most young teens begin to experiment with the degree of individuality or conformity they are comfortable with.

It is not surprising that this is about the age when the curriculum begins to encourage students to ask questions about identity and self-acceptance. That is, in fact, the final step. We see this emerging most profoundly in grades 8 and 9.

As you saw in the table on the previous page, students in grade 8 (12, 13, and 14 years old) are expected to "understand and accept" their gender identity and sexual orientation. The presupposition, of course, is that this is something that needs to be understood – something is unclear. This also assumes that kids have the physical and emotional maturity to make such a decision if something is unclear. It brings decision-making about gender identity and sexual orientation into the classroom and – and in my opinion – plants ideas in the minds of children who did not have any thought of questioning their sexuality or gender.

In grade 9, the final year of mandatory health education in the public system, students "demonstrate an understanding of factors that can influence a person's understanding of their gender identity and sexual orientation, and identify sources of support for all students."[9] Interestingly, further dialogue on these topics dies out after grade 9 – the curriculum is silent on the subject in grade 10, 11 and 12. So the final word gets spoken in grade 9, and it is loud and clear.

Students ask, "What is my gender identity? Male? Female? Two-spirited? Transgender? Gender-fluid? Maybe no gender at all?"

The curriculum responds, "Your gender identity is based on your own sense of self. It may be different from your biological or birth-assigned sex."

Students ask, "What is my sexual orientation? Heterosexual? Gay? Lesbian? Bisexual? Pansexual? Asexual? Skoliosexual?"[a]

The curriculum responds, "Your sexual orientation comes from how you think of yourself in terms of your sexual and romantic attraction to others."[10]

Students ask, "What is my sense of self? Who am I?" and the curriculum leads the student to believe that they are the author of their own identity. They get the final word.

Self-Image and Self-Concept

You'll notice the focus is on the importance of the *self*: Be self-aware. Have a good self-concept. Accept yourself.

The curriculum defines self-concept as "the perception a person has of his or her own identity. People form their self-concept using interpretations of information they acquire about themselves through experiences and interactions with others and their environment."[11]

Note that self-concept is formed by experiences and interactions with others, not by individual action or behaviour. Self-concept, according to the curriculum, is less about "Who I think I am" but more of "Who others say I am."

---

[a] The list of sexual orientations as of this writing is widely varied, depending on the source. Just google "how many sexual orientations are there?" and you'll see what I mean.

There are about twelve references to self-concept in the curriculum. Three are in relation to how one's sexuality or gender identity can affect one's self-concept. Three are in relation to actions a student can take to positively affect their self-concept with suggestions such as healthy eating and exercise, fostering a positive attitude, acknowledging one's strengths and skills, and developing a sense of purpose. These are all great suggestions. However, *six of the twelve* references to self-concept in the curriculum focus on the role of others in creating a negative or positive self-concept.

Six out of twelve occurrences is a lot. This leads me to the conclusion that children are being taught that how others view them makes as much of an impact on their self-concept and ultimately, their self-worth, than who they know themselves to be. The emphasis is not placed on students doing their best in school or engaging in skill and character building activities and generally positively contributing to society. The emphasis, and the impetus, is put on others to be the defining factor in whether a student has a positive or negative self-concept and how to cope with this input.

When the curriculum advocates for a positive self-concept, it doesn't consider that someone could recognize that they experience same-sex attraction or a draw to cross-gender expression, yet reject the temptation to express it. Instead, the culture and curriculum insist that a person's self-concept can only "develop positively if a person understands and accepts their gender identity and sexual orientation"[12] and is accepted as such by others.

Remember the "milestone progression" we discussed in chapter two? The curriculum – and the culture as a whole – goes one step further. It says that if I feel a certain way, I need to admit it, act on it, proclaim it, embrace it and finally, demand everyone else accept it.

We live in a time when kids are basing their value on how many Facebook shares, Instagram likes, or YouTube subscribers they get. This emphasis on others' opinions is the last thing they need to hear.

Students need to be told that their value comes from how unique they are as a person who bears the image of God,[b] not from whether or not they are accepted by their peers. They need to be encouraged to develop their strengths, work on their weaknesses, and build relationships with people of common interests. They need to know that the opinions of others, both positive and negative, should be considered in the light of whether they align to the truth as stated in God's Word. They need to be able to identify and reject a lie that is spoken to them about who they are.

Most importantly they need to know that their self-concept, their identity, needs to be rooted in the opinion of the one who created them and he says they are fearfully and wonderfully made,[c] created for a purpose,[d] and his beloved child.[e] There is danger in becoming too obsessed or focused on ourselves. We forget that we are sinful and that God is holy. We trust ourselves and our feelings rather than the authority of God's Word.

Created for a Purpose

When a student has been "raised" on comprehensive sex education, they are taught that it's very important to wonder about their sexuality and more recently, their gender.

Our kids absolutely need to understand and accept their identity. But the question is not about their gender or sexuality, the question is about whose acceptance really matters.

We cannot let the culture have the final word. Parents, church leaders, and Christian teachers, these are *our* children and this is *our* chance to be certain that the first and final word they hear about

---

[b] Genesis 1:26-27
[c] Psalm 139
[d] Ephesians 2:10
[e] John 3:16

their identity is from God's word. Our children need us there every step of the way, affirming and instructing them in who they are in Christ, who God says they are, their true identity.

As we (Char and I, with our friend Kim Hanson) thought about and discussed the potential impact the culture and school curriculums could have on our kids, God convicted us of the need to equip parents to intentionally counter the harmful messages our kids are receiving from the world. We believe that it is critical for parents to be the ones who introduce their kids to these topics: sexuality, including homosexuality and the world's views about sex; and gender, including the world's views about self. Along with that, we need to get our kids deeply familiar with God's Word on the same topics. We need to open the conversation and leave it open so that our children feel free to jump in at any time with a question, experience, or feeling that they want to work through with us.

Look for *Created for a Purpose*, a resource for children ages 5-9, coming later in 2017.

But that's only part of the conversation, albeit an important part. We have come to believe that what is truly critical is that we instill in our kids a sense of awe over their design and creation by an Almighty Creator God: a deep, abiding wonder as they come to understand that God has placed his fingerprints on them along with his divine stamp of approval.

This task can easily seem overwhelming. Thankfully, we are not in it alone. God has promised us that when we are walking in his will and doing his work, we have the empowerment of the Holy

Spirit. *We* are created for a purpose and have specific "good things" that God has given us to do![f] In fact, before we begin this task of speaking into our children's lives, we need to accept and understand this truth for ourselves! Among the good things God has given us to do is raising our children to understand that they also have purpose and tasks of their own. We also need to recognize that God has equipped us with everything we need to do this work.[g]

The best approach is to build a solid, biblical foundation with your children. If you and your family have firmly established your beliefs, and understand the Scriptures that back them up, you will be in a much better position to identify things that are harmful or false. As much as we wish Biblical values and truths would be absorbed by breathing the air in our homes, this will not happen. We must be intentional.

We've given this a lot of thought and prayer and God has led us to begin developing a companion series called *Created for a Purpose*. This resource contains lessons that are designed to help you establish a foundation for your child's identity in Christ. The lessons are developed around the key verse mentioned above, "For we are God's masterpiece. He has created us anew in Christ Jesus, so we can do the good things he planned for us long ago."[h]

Within *Created for a Purpose*, we will go over key messages from God's Word to help children understand who they are in Christ. The lessons are timed so that they correspond with what children are learning at school and can create a foundation within them that will help them properly interpret what they are learning. Here is an outline of some of the lessons we plan to include:

---

[f] Ephesians 2:10
[g] 2 Peter 1:3
[h] Ephesians 2:10

Speaking the Truth into Your Child's Identity

At school they are learning	Their true identity in Christ
Grade 1 • Naming body parts, including genitalia	• I am God's masterpiece! (God's purpose for creation, God's purpose for people, God's purpose for me) • I am wonderfully made • I cannot be separated from God's love
Grade 2 • Stages of growth (the body) • Diverse family structures (Social Studies)	• I have new life in Christ • I am becoming more like Jesus • I am precious to God • I am accepted • God's plan for marriage
Grade 3 • "Visible and invisible differences" including gender identity, gender expression, and sexual orientation	• I can do the good things God planned for me to do • I have everything I need to fulfill my purpose (gifts, talents, personality, gender, etc.) • I am created in God's image (God's design for male and female) • Everyone has value

Grounding your child in these truths will empower them to understand how God sees them. The hope is that being rooted in the truth of God's Word, your child will be able to apply what they've learned to situations she or he encounters and be able to critically assess what they are being taught or are seeing through the lens of God's Word.

Can you imagine the impact on a child's self-image when he truly understands that he is God's masterpiece, created with a heavenly to-do list that only he is capable of fulfilling? That all of heaven gathered around after God created him saying in awe, "Creator, You've done it again. A masterpiece!" Our goal is to set you up for meaningful, rich discussions with your children about how they can hold firmly to their beliefs in an increasingly ungodly world.

The promises in God's Word are rich for the work ahead of you and the outcome in your child! Psalm 1:1-3 says,

> Oh, the joys of those who do not
> > follow the advice of the wicked,
> > or stand around with sinners,
> > or join in with mockers.
> But they delight in the law of the Lord,
> > meditating on it day and night.
> They are like trees planted along the riverbank,
> > bearing fruit each season.
> Their leaves never wither,
> > and they prosper in all they do.

---

[1] Ontario, Ministry of Education, *The Ontario Curriculum, Grades 1-8: Health and Physical Education,* 93.
[2] Ibid., 124.
[3] Ibid., 158-9.
[4] Ibid., 172.
[5] Ibid., 162.
[6] Ibid., 215.
[7] Ibid., emphasis mine.

[8] Ibid., emphasis mine.
[9] Ontario, Ministry of Education, *The Ontario Curriculum, Grades 9-12: Health and Physical Education*, 104.
[10] Ibid., pronouns changed from third person to second person.
[11] Ibid., 215.
[12] Ontario, Ministry of Education, *The Ontario Curriculum, Grades 1-8: Health and Physical Education*, 216

Appendix

The Ontario Curriculum: Addressing Barriers to Acceptance of Sexual Orientation, Gender Identity, and Gender Expression

The expectations, teacher prompts, and student responses are summarized briefly here in order to show the progressive nature of instruction. You are strongly encouraged to access the public curriculum documents and read the pertinent sections for yourself. Information on where to find the specific information is in the endnotes of this chapter.

Grade 1

Prior Knowledge, Self-Awareness

Children are taught names of male and female genitalia. (C1.3)[1]

NOTE: While not assigned this purpose within the curriculum, knowledge of genitalia is required in order to understand gender identity and sexual orientation and, we believe, is one of the primary purposes for its inclusion for such young children.

Grade 2

Stereotypes

(Social Studies) Same-sex families are one of many types of families.[2]

Grade 3

Stigma, Stereotypes, Self-Awareness

Self-awareness is a factor in my emotional development [3]

Gender identity and sexual orientation are an invisible difference that makes a person unique. We need to show respect for the differences in others.[4]

Grade 5

Self-Image, Culture (Family)

Conflict between personal desires and cultural teachings and practices can cause stress during puberty. Accessing information about your concerns helps manage stress.

Student response: "Things I can control include being open to new ideas; whether I make my own decisions or let myself be influenced by others ... Things I cannot control include whether I am male or female, my gender identity, sexual orientation ..."[5]

Self-Concept, Stigma, Stereotypes

A person's actions can affect their own and others' feelings, self-concept, emotional well-being, and reputation (e.g., "homophobic remarks")

Teacher prompt: "Negative actions can hurt others and result in stigma ... we may view [someone who has HIV or a mental health problem] in a stereotyped manner and make assumptions. Stereotypes can have a strong, negative impact on someone's self-concept and well-being."[6]

Grade 6

Stereotypes, Self-Awareness

Stereotypes, homophobia and assumptions about gender roles and expectations, sexual orientation, gender expression, etc. affect an individual's self-concept, social inclusion, and relationships with others.[7]

Teacher prompt: Assumptions about what's normal for males/females/sexual orientation are "usually untrue and can be harmful ... Assumptions about different sexual orientations or about people with learning disabilities or mental illness or about people from other cultures are harmful in similar ways."[8]

Grade 7

Self-Awareness, Culture, Religion, Stigma

When making decisions about sexual health ("whether to have sex or wait"), consider gender identity, sexual orientation, cultural teachings, religious beliefs, and moral considerations.[9]

The truth about HIV is downplayed: "One of the best things you can do to stop HIV is to stop the stigma that is associated with it."[10]

Grade 8

Self-Awareness, Acceptance, Religion, Culture, Media

Factors that can affect an individual's decisions about sexual activity include awareness and acceptance of gender identity and sexual orientation, religious beliefs, cultural information, media messages, etc.[11]

Demonstrate an understanding of gender identity, gender expression, and sexual orientation, as well as how these are connected to your self-concept. Sources of support are explored.[12]

Grade 9

All identified factors directly addressed, specifically Culture and Religion

Factors that can influence a person's understanding of their gender identity, gender expression, and sexual orientation are addressed as acceptance, stigma, culture, religion, media, stereotypes, homophobia, self-image, self-awareness. [13]

> *Student response:* "A person's sense of self is affected by the person's cultural and family background, religion, and what they have come to value. Media images, role models, support systems, and acceptance or lack of acceptance by others could influence how different people feel about their gender identity or sexual orientation." "Expectations or assumptions about masculinity and femininity and about heterosexuality as the norm can affect the self-image of those who do not fit those expectations or assumptions. This can make it difficult for a person to feel accepted by others." [14]

Students can be supported in their gender identity or sexual orientation by talking to others who may be dealing with the same issues: LGBTQ community organizations, gay-straight alliances, guidance counsellors, health professionals, trusted adults, and friends, etc. [15]

Grade 10

Culture, Religion, Homophobia

Misconceptions about sexuality in our culture may cause harm to people. These can be based on erroneous information. [16]

Heterosexism affects those who are questioning their sexual orientation or gender identity. [17]

Appendix

Ontario's curriculum documents are freely available online and can be found by searching "Ontario Ministry of Education Curriculum" or at http://www.edu.gov.on.ca/eng/teachers/curriculum.html.

[1] Ontario, Ministry of Education, *The Ontario Curriculum, Grades 1-8: Health and Physical Education*, 93.
[2] Ontario, Ministry of Education, *The Ontario Curriculum / Social Studies, Grades 1 to 6; History and Geography, Grades 7 and 8*, 78.
[3] Ontario, Ministry of Education, *The Ontario Curriculum, Grades 1-8: Health and Physical Education*, 122.
[4] Ibid., 124.
[5] Ibid., 158-9.
[6] Ibid., 160.
[7] Ibid., 172, 177.
[8] Ibid., 177.
[9] Ibid., 199.
[10] Ibid., 197.
[11] Ibid., 215.
[12] Ibid., 216.
[13] Ontario, Ministry of Education, *The Ontario Curriculum, Grades 9 to 12: Health and Physical Education*, 104.
[14] Ibid., 104.
[15] Ibid.
[16] Ibid., 126.
[17] Ibid

Bibliography

"About Us." *OPHEA.net*. Accessed January 26, 2017. https://www.ophea.net/about-us.

"Accept." *Dictionary.com*, April 11, 2015. http://dictionary.reference.com/browse/accept?s=t.

"Adolescent and School Health | Sexual Risk Behaviors: : HIV, STD, & Teen Pregnancy Prevention." Accessed January 27, 2017. https://www.cdc.gov/healthyyouth/sexualbehaviors/.

Alphonso, Caroline. "When Ms. Straughan Became Mr. Straughan: How a Transgender Teacher Learned to Be Himself - The Globe and Mail." *Gobe and Mail*. April 22, 2016. http://www.theglobeandmail.com/news/toronto/when-ms-straughan-became-mr-straughan-how-a-transgender-teacher-learned-to-be-himself/article29726503/.

Ast, David, Michael Erickson, Deborah Gladstone, Amy Gottlieb, Richard Ng, and Jennifer Parkins. *Challenging Homophobia and Heterosexism: A K-12 Curriculum Resource Guide*. Toronto District School Board, 2011.

Baklinski, Pete. "Lesbian: I Use Math Class to Teach Young Kids about Homosexuality so I Can 'hide' It from Parents." *LifeSiteNews*, April 24, 2015. https://www.lifesitenews.com/news/lesbian-i-use-math-class-to-teach-young-kids-about-homosexuality-so-i-can-h.

Bergman, Jerry. "Kinsey, Darwin and the Sexual Revolution -." *Journal of Creation* 20, no. 3 (December 2006): 111–17.

Berry, Kristen. "Gender Differences in Teenagers." *Our Everyday Life*, 2017. http://oureverydaylife.com/gender-differences-teenagers-16388.html.

Boekeloo, B. O. and D. E. Howard. "Oral Sexual Experience among Young Adolescents Receiving General Health Examinations. - PubMed - NCBI." *American Journal of Health Behaviour* 26, no. 4 (August 2002): 306–14.

Bohlin, Sue. "The Gender Spectrum." *Probe for Answers*, January 7, 2011. https://www.probe.org/the-gender-spectrum/.

Brizendine, Louann. *The Female Brain*. New York: Broadway Books, 2006.

Brody, Jane. "Boyhood Effeminacy and Later Homosexuality." *New York Times*, December 16, 1986. http://www.nytimes.com/1986/12/16/science/boyhood-effeminancy-and-later-homosexuality.html?pagewanted=1.

Browder, Sue Ellin. "Kinsey's Secret: The Phony Science of the Sexual Revolution." *Crisis Magazine*, May 28, 2012. http://www.crisismagazine.com/2012/kinseys-secret-the-phony-science-of-the-sexual-revolution.

Canada. "Canadian Community Health Survey - Annual Component (CCHS)." *Statistics Canada*, June 24, 2016. http://www23.statcan.gc.ca/imdb/p2SV.pl?Function=getSurvey&SDDS=3226.

Canada. "Portrait of Families and Living Arrangements in Canada." *Statistics Canada*. Accessed September 22, 2015. http://www12.statcan.ca/census-recensement/2011/as-sa/98-312-x/98-312-x2011001-eng.cfm#a4.

Canada. Ontario. "Gender Identity and Gender Expression | Ontario Human Rights Commission." Government. *Ontario Human Rights Commission*. Accessed January 24, 2017. http://www.ohrc.on.ca/en/code_grounds/gender_identity.

Canada. Ontario. *Policy on Discrimination and Harassment Because of Sexual Orientation*. Queen's Printer for Ontario, 2006. http://www.ohrc.on.ca/sites/default/files/attachments/Policy_on_discrimination_and_harassment_because_of_sexual_orientation.pdf.

Canada. Ontario. *Policy on Preventing Discrimination and Harassment because of Gender Identity and Gender Expression. 5. Emerging Human Rights Protections*. Queen's Printer for Ontario, 2014. http://www.ohrc.on.ca/en/policy-preventing-discrimination-because-gender-identity-and-gender-expression/5-emerging-human-rights-protections.

Canada. Ontario. "The Ontario Human Rights Code." Ontario Human Rights Canada. Ontario. , December 5, 2016. http://du0tsrdospf80.cloudfront.net/docs/90h19_e.doc.

Canada. Ontario. "OHRC Remarks to the Ontario Legislative Standing Committee on Social Policy Regarding Bill 13 and Bill 14." Ontario Human Rights Commission, 2012. http://www.ohrc.on.ca/en/ohrc-remarks-ontario-legislative-standing-committee-social-policy-regarding-bill-13-and-bill-14.

Canada. Ontario. Ministry of Education. "The Ontario Curriculum: Elementary | Frequently Asked Questions: What Are Curriculum Documents?" *Ontario Ministry of Education*, November 16, 2016. http://www.edu.gov.on.ca/eng/curriculum/elementary/common.html#display

Canada. Ontario. Ministry of Education. *The Ontario Curriculum, Grades 9-12: Health and Physical Education*. Toronto, Ontario: Queen's Printer for Ontario, 2015. http://www.edu.gov.on.ca/eng/curriculum/secondary/health9to12.pdf.

Canada. Ontario. Ministry of Education. "Creating Safe and Accepting Schools: Information for Parents about the Accepting Schools Act (Bill 13)." Ontario Ministry of Education, 2012. http://www.edu.gov.on.ca/eng/safeschools/SafeAccepSchools.pd.

Canada. Ontario. Ministry of Education. "Policy/Program Memorandum No. 145: Progressive Discipline and Promoting Positive Student Behaviour." Ontario Ministry of Education, 2012. http://www.edu.gov.on.ca/extra/eng/ppm/145.pdf.

Canada. Ontario. Ministry of Education. *Realizing the Promise of Diversity: Ontario's Equity and Inclusive Education Strategy*. Toronto, Ontario: Queen's Printer for Ontario. Accessed January 24, 2017. http://www.edu.gov.on.ca/eng/policyfunding/equity.pdf.

Canada. Ontario. Ministry of Education. *The Ontario Curriculum | Social Studies, Grades 1 to 6; History and Geography, Grades 7 and 8*. Toronto, Ontario: Queen's Printer for Ontario, 2013. http://www.edu.gov.on.ca/eng/curriculum/elementary/sshg18curr2013.pdf.

Canada. Ontario. Ministry of Education *The Ontario Curriculum, Grades 1-8, Language*. Toronto, Ontario: Queen's Printer for Ontario, 2006. http://www.edu.gov.on.ca/eng/curriculum/elementary/language18currb.pdf.

Bibliography

Canada. Ontario. Ministry of Education *The Ontario Curriculum, Grades 1-8: The Arts*. Toronto, Ontario: Queen's Printer for Ontario, 2009. http://www.edu.gov.on.ca/eng/curriculum/elementary/arts18b09curr.pdf.

Canada. Ontario. Ministry of Education. *The Ontario Curriculum, Grades 1-8: Health and Physical Education*. Toronto, Ontario: Queen's Printer for Ontario, 2015. http://www.edu.gov.on.ca/eng/curriculum/elementary/health1to8.pdf.

Canada. Public Health Agency of Canada. "HIV/AIDS Epi Updates: National HIV Prevalence and Incidence Estimates for 2011." *Centre for Communicable Diseases and Infection Control, Public Health Agency of Canada*, November 28, 2014. http://www.phac-aspc.gc.ca/aids-sida/publication/epi/2010/1-eng.php#a0503.

"Canada Watch: A Word from the President, Bruce J. Clemenger." *Evangelical Fellowship of Canada,* January 2017. http://files.efc-canada.net/efc/newsletters/canadawatch/CW2016Dec.pdf.

Centers for Disease Control and Prevention, "STDs in Men Who Have Sex with Men," *Centers for Disease Control and Prevention,* November 11, 2011. https://www.cdc.gov/std/stats10/msm.htm.

Centers for Disease Control and Prevention, "Sexually Transmitted Diseases," *Centers for Disease Control and Prevention,* March 9, 2016. https://www.cdc.gov/msmhealth/std.htm.

Centers for Disease Control and Prevention, "Viral Hepatitis," *Centers for Disease Control and Prevention,* February 29, 2016. https://www.cdc.gov/msmhealth/viral-hepatitis.htm.

Centers for Disease Control and Prevention, "HIV Among Transgender People," *Centers for Disease Control and Prevention*, April 2016, https://www.cdc.gov/hiv/pdf/group/gender/transgender/cdc-hiv-transgender.pdf.

Challacombe, L. "The Epidemiology of HIV in Canada." *CATIE*, 2017. http://www.catie.ca/en/fact-sheets/epidemiology/epidemiology-hiv-canada.

Challacombe, L. "The Epidemiology of HIV in Gay Men and Other Men Who have Sex with Men." *CATIE*, 2017. http://www.catie.ca/fact-sheets/epidemiology/epidemiology-hiv-gay-men-and-other-men-who-have-sex-men.

Challacombe, L. "The Epidemiology of HIV in Youth." *CATIE*, 2015. http://www.catie.ca/en/fact-sheets/epidemiology/epidemiology-hiv- youth.

Chung, W. C., G. J. De Vries, and D. F. Swaab. "Sexual Differentiation of the Bed Nucleus of the Stria Terminalis in Humans May Extend into Adulthood." *The Journal of Neuroscience* 22, no. 3 (February 1, 2002): 1027–33.

Ciccoritti, Jerry. "Honeymoon." *Schitt's Creek*. CBC, 2015.

Colapinto, John. "The True Story of John / Joan." *Rolling Stone*, December 11, 1997.

Coleman, E., W. Bockting, P. Cohen-Kettenis, G. DeCuypere, and J. Feldman. "Standards of Care for the Health of Transsexual, Transgender, and Gender-

Nonconforming People, Version 7." *International Journal of Transgenderism* 13, no. 4 (2012): 165–232. doi:10.1080/15532739.2011.700873.

Collins, Clare, and Lisa Rossi. "Rectal Microbicides Fact Sheet." *Microbicide Trials Network*, August 11, 2016. http://www.mtnstopshiv.org/node/2864.

"Comprehensive Sexuality Education (CSE): Sexual Rights vs. Sexual Health." Family Watch International. Accessed January 26, 2017.
http://www.familywatchinternational.org/fwi/documents/fwipolicybriefCSE.pdf.

"Condom Fact Sheet In Brief | Condom Effectiveness." *Centers for Disease Control and Prevention*, March 5, 2013.
https://www.cdc.gov/condomeffectiveness/brief.html.

Crosby, R. A., R. J. DiClemente, G. M. Wingwood, D. Lang, and K. F. Harrington. "Value of Consistent Condom Use: A Study of Sexually Transmitted Disease Prevention among African American Adolescent Females." *American Journal of Public Health* 93, no. 6 (June 2003): 901–2.

"Curve Magazine - North America's Best-Selling Lesbian Magazine." Accessed July 5, 2015. http://www.curvemag.com/.

"Daily Xtra | Gay & Lesbian News." Accessed July 5, 2015. http://www.dailyxtra.com/.

Daly, Jim. "Navigating Sexual Sin to Find Your Identity in Christ (Part 2 of 2)." *Focus on the Family Daily Broadcast*. Colorado Springs, January 11, 2017.
http://www.focusonthefamily.com/media/daily-broadcast/navigating-sexual-sin-to-find-your-identity-in-christ-pt2.

DeHaan, Linda. *King and King*. Berkley, California: Tricycle Press, 2002.
https://www.amazon.ca/King-Linda-Haan/dp/1582460612.

Dhejne, Cecilia, Paul Lichtenstein, Marcus Boman, Anna L. V. Johansson, Niklas Langstrom, and Mikael Landen. "Long-Term Follow-Up of Transsexual Persons Undergoing Sex Reassignment Surgery: Cohort Study in Sweden." Edited by James Scott. *PLoS ONE*, e16885, 6, no. 2 (February 22, 2011).
doi:10.1371/journal.pone.0016885.

Diamond, Milton, and H. Keith Sigmundson. "Sex Reassignment at Birth: A Long Term Review and Clinical Implications." *Archives of Pediatrics and Adolescent Medicine* 151 (March 1997).
http://www.hawaii.edu/PCSS/biblio/articles/1961to1999/1997-sex-reassignment.html.

DiNovo, Cheri. Affirming Sexual Orientation and Gender Identity Act, 2015, Pub. L. No. 77, § 11.2. Accessed January 25, 2017.
http://www.ontla.on.ca/web/bills/bills_detail.do?locale=en&BillID=319.

Drummond, Kelley D., Susan J. Bradley, Michele Peterson-Badali, and Kenneth J. Zucker. "A Follow-up Study of Girls with Gender Identity Disorder." *Developmental Psychology* 44, no. 1 (January 2008): 34–45. doi:10.1037/0012-1649.44.1.34.

"Edmonton Catholic School Bans Transgender Child, 7, from Girls' Washroom." *CBCNews, Edmonton*, May 14, 2015.
http://www.cbc.ca/news/canada/edmonton/edmonton-catholic-school-bans-transgender-child-7-from-girls-washroom-1.3073737.

Bibliography

"Equipping Parents to Respond to Gender-Confusing Messages in Schools." Focus on the Family. Accessed January 25, 2017. http://focusonthefamily.com/EmpowerParents.

Ewert, Robert, *10,000 Dresses*, New York: Triangle Square, 2008.

Fethers, K.; Marks, Caron; Mindel, Adrian; Estcourt, Claudia S., "Sexually Transmitted Infections and Risk Behaviors in Women Who Have Sex with Women, "*Sexually Transmitted Infections* 76 (2000).

Flores, Andrew R., Jody L. Herman, Gary J. Gates, and Taylor N. T. Brown. "How Many Adults Identify as Transgender in the United States?" The Williams Institute, June 2016. http://williamsinstitute.law.ucla.edu/wp-content/uploads/How-Many-Adults-Identify-as-Transgender-in-the-United-States.pdf.

"For the Love of Learning | Volume II: Learning - Our Vision for Schools Chapter 11: Evaluating Achievement." Queen's Printer for Ontario, 1994. http://www.edu.gov.on.ca/eng/general/abcs/rcom/full/volume2/chapter11.htm.

Forbes, John C., Ariane M. Alimenti, Joel Singer, Jason C. Brophy, Ari Bitnun, Lindy M. Samson, Deborah M. Money, Terry C.K. Lee, Normand D. Lapointe, and Stanley E. Read. "A National Review of Vertical HIV Transmission:" *AIDS* 26, no. 6 (March 2012): 757–63. doi:10.1097/QAD.0b013e328350995c.

Gaffield, Chad. "History of Education - The Canadian Encyclopedia." *Historica Canada*, March 4, 2015. http://www.thecanadianencyclopedia.ca/en/article/history-of-education/.

Gale, Kimberley. "HIV Killer Ruled Dangerous Offender." *CBC News, Canada*, August 2, 2011. http://www.cbc.ca/news/canada/hiv-killer-ruled-dangerous-offender-1.927621.

Gandolfo, Frederick. "Does Anal Sex Cause Fecal Incontinence?" *Gastroenterology & Endoscopy News*, February 25, 2016. http://www.gastroendonews.com/Retroflexions/Article/03-15/Does-anal-sex-cause-fecal-incontinence-/35422.

Garden, Nancy, and Sharon Wooding. *Molly's Family*. Farrar, Straus and Giroux, 2004.

Garofalo, Robert. "The Association Between Health Risk Behaviors and Sexual Orientation Among a School-Based Sample of Adolescents." *Pediatrics* 101, no. 5 (1998): 895–902.

Gates, Gary J. "How Many People Are Lesbian, Gay, Bisexual, and Transgender?" The Williams Institute, April 2011. http://williamsinstitute.law.ucla.edu/wp-content/uploads/Gates-How-Many-People-LGBT-Apr-2011.pdf.

Gattis, Maurice N., Woodford, Michael R., and Han, Yoonsun. Archives of Sex Behavior, 43, no. 8, (2014: 1589–1599), https://www.ncbi.nlm.nih.gov/pmc/articles/PMC4507415/

"Gay and Bisexual Men's Health: Sexually Transmitted Diseases." *Centers for Disease Control and Prevention*, March 9, 2016. https://www.cdc.gov/msmhealth/STD.htm.

"Gender Definitions." *Trans-Parenting*. Accessed January 27, 2017. http://www.trans-parenting.com/understanding-gender/gender-definitions/.

Goldberg, Joseph. "Gender Dysphoria: What It Is and How It's Treated." *WebMD*, September 9, 2016. http://www.webmd.com/mental-health/gender-dysphoria#1.

Gosselin, J., E. Romano, L. Babchishin, T. Bell, I. Hudon-ven der Buhs, A. Gagne, and N. Gosselin. "Canadian Portrait of Changes in Family Structure and Pre-School Children's Behavioral Outcomes. Vol. 38, Iss. 6, P. 523." *International Journal of Behavioral Development*, 2014, 38, no. 6 (2014): 523.

Graaf, R de, Theo G. M. Sandfort, and M ten Have. "Suicidality and Sexual Orientation: Differences between Men and Women in a General Population-Based Sample from the Netherlands." *Archives of Sexual Behavior* 35, no. 3 (2006): 253–62.

Grossman, Miriam. "About." *Miriam Grossman, MD*. Accessed January 26, 2017. http://www.miriamgrossmanmd.com/about/.

Grossman, Miriam. *You're Teaching My Child What?* Washington, D.C.: Regnery Publishing, Inc., 2009.

Grossman, Miriam. "You're Teaching My Child What? The Truth About Sex Education." *Heritage*, August 9, 2010. http://www.heritage.org/research/lecture/youre-teaching-my-child-what-the-truth-about-sex-education.

Hamzelou, Jessica. "Transsexual Differences Caught on Brain Scan." *New Scientist*, January 26, 2011. https://www.newscientist.com/article/dn20032-transsexual-differences-caught-on-brain-scan.

"Hands Up!: Identifying Parents' Rights in the Education System; A Discussion Paper on Understanding the Rights and Responsibilities of Parents, Children, Education Institutions and Government." The Evangelical Fellowship of Canada. Accessed January 26, 2017. http://files.efccanada.net/si/Education/HandsUpIdentifyingParentsRights2010.pdf.

Hare, Lauren, Pascal Bernard, Francisco J. Sánchez, Paul N. Baird, Eric Vilain, Trudy Kennedy, and Vincent R. Harley. "Androgen Receptor Repeat Length Polymorphism Associated with Male-to-Female Transsexualism." *Biological Psychiatry* 65, no. 1 (January 1, 2009): 93–96. doi:10.1016/j.biopsych.2008.08.033.

"Health Implications Associated with Homosexuality." The Medical Institute for Sexual Health, 1999. http://www.ccv.org/wp-content/uploads/2010/04/MISH1.pdf.

Hequembourg, Amy L. and Dearing, Ronda L. "Exploring Shame, Guilt, and Risky Substance Use among Sexual Minority Men and Women" Journal of Homosexuality, 60, no. 4 (2013:615–638), https://www.ncbi.nlm.nih.gov/pmc/articles/PMC3621125/.

Heyer, Walt. "I Was a Transgender Woman | Public Discourse." *The Witherspoon Institute: Public Discourse*, April 1, 2015. http://www.thepublicdiscourse.com/2015/04/14688/.

Heyer, Walt. "Public School LGBT Programs Don't Just Trample Parental Rights. They Also Put Kids at Risk." *The Witherspoon Institute: Public Discourse*, June 8, 2015. http://www.thepublicdiscourse.com/2015/06/15118/.

Hiemstra, Rick. "Ontario Health Curriculum: Parent Resource," October 1, 2015.

Highleyman, Liz. "Just How Risky Is It? Studies Shed Light on HIV Risk and Prevention." *BetaBlog*, June 4, 2014. http://betablog.org/studies-shed-light-on-hiv-risk-and-prevention/.

Bibliography

"HIV & AIDS Information :: Condoms and Lubricants - Do Condoms Work?" *Aidsmap*, 2017. http://www.aidsmap.com/Do-condoms-work/page/1746203/.

"HIV Among Transgender People." Centers for Disease Control and Prevention, April 2016. https://www.cdc.gov/hiv/pdf/group/gender/transgender/cdc-hiv-transgender.pdf.

"HIV in the United States: At A Glance." *Centers for Disease Control and Prevention*, December 2, 2016. https://www.cdc.gov/hiv/statistics/overview/ataglance.html.

"HIV Stigma and Discrimination." *Canadian Aids Society,* Accessed May 12, 2016. http://www.cdnaids.ca/files.nsf/pages/HIV-Stigma-and-discriminati/$file/CAS_WAD_InfoSheet_HIVStigma_EN.pdf.

Hogg, R., Strathdee, S., Craib, K., O'Shaughnessy, M., Montaner, J., and Schechter, M. "Modelling the Impact of HIV Disease on Mortality in Gay and Bisexual Men." *International Journal of Epidemiology* 26, no. 3 (June 1, 1997): 657–61. doi:10.1093/ije/26.3.657.

Hottes, Travis Salway, Olivier Ferlatte, and Dionne Gesink. "Suicide and HIV as Leading Causes of Death among Gay and Bisexual Men: A Comparison of Estimated Mortality and Published Research: Critical Public Health: Vol 25, No 5." *Critical Public Health* 25, no. 5 (March 26, 2014): 513–26. doi:10.1080/09581596.2014.946887.

Canada. Parliament. House of Commons. An Act to amend the Canadian Human Rights Act and the Criminal Code, Pub. L. No. C-16 (2015). http://www.parl.gc.ca/HousePublications/Publication.aspx?Language=E&Mode=1&DocId=8609176.

"How Do You Eliminate Guilt and Shame Associated with Being Transgender?" Forum. *Crossdressers: The #1 Community for Crossdressers, Their Family and Friends*, May 14, 2012. https://www.crossdressers.com/forums/showthread.php?174254-How-do-you-eliminate-guilt-and-shame-associated-with-being-transgender.

"HPV, Anal Dysplasia and Anal Cancer." *CATIE - Canada's Source for HIV and Hepatitis C Information*, 2016. http://www.catie.ca/en/fact-sheets/cancers/hpv-anal-dysplasia-and-anal-cancer.

"Human Papillomavirus (HPV) Vaccines." *National Cancer Institute*, November 2, 2016. https://www.cancer.gov/about-cancer/causes-prevention/risk/infectious-agents/hpv-vaccine-fact-sheet.

"'I Am a Woman Now, but I Really Hate Women Sometimes.'" *Transgender Reality: What Trans People Are Really Saying Online*. Accessed January 25, 2017. https://transgenderreality.com/tag/jealousy/.

"Identity." Merriam-Webster. Accessed January 25, 2017. https://www.merriam-webster.com/dictionary/identity.

"Indoctrinate." *Merriam-Webster*, 2017. https://www.merriam-webster.com/dictionary/indoctrinate.

itssosoph. *Being Transgender and Jealousy*. Accessed January 25, 2017. https://www.youtube.com/watch?v=Zf9lWU9E0BM&feature=youtu.be.

Jolly, Kathleen. "Reality Check: What's the Evidence behind Ontario's Sex Ed Curriculum? | Globalnews.ca." *Global News*. March 4, 2015.

http://globalnews.ca/news/1863258/reality-check-whats-the-evidence-behind-ontarios-sex-ed-curriculum/.

"Just Say Yes: Respect." *Coalition for Positive Sexuality*, 1997. http://www.positive.org/JustSayYes/respect.html.

Kaltenbach, Caleb. *Messy Grace*. Colorado Springs: Water Brook Press, 2015.

Kaplan, Ami. "Some Thoughts on Shame and Being Transgender." *Transgender Mental Health*, January 1, 2013. https://tgmentalhealth.com/2013/01/01/some-thoughts-on-shame-and-being-transgender/.

Kay, Barbara. "Barbara Kay: Bill 77, the Affirming Sexual Orientation and Gender Identity Act, is a Dangerous Overreach | National Post." *National Post*, June 2, 2015. http://news.nationalpost.com/full-comment/barbara-kay-bill-77-the-affirming-sexual-orientation-and-gender-identity-act-is-a-dangerous-overreach.

Killerman, Sam. "Comprehensive* List of LGBTQ+ Vocabulary Definitions." *It's Pronounced METROsexual*. Accessed January 27, 2017. http://itspronouncedmetrosexual.com/2013/01/a-comprehensive-list-of-lgbtq-term-definitions/#sthash.lofZmUJM.dpbs.

Killerman, Sam. "The Genderbread Person v3." *It's Pronounced METROsexual*, 2015. http://itspronouncedmetrosexual.com/2015/03/the-genderbread-person-v3/.

Kilman, Carrie. "The Gender Spectrum | Teaching Tolerance - Diversity, Equity and Justice." *Teaching Tolerance: A Project of the Southern Poverty Law Center*, Summer 2013. http://www.tolerance.org/gender-spectrum.

Kinsey, Alfred. "Sexual Behaviour in the Human Male." *Kinsey Institute*, 1948. http://www.kinseyinstitute.org/resources/bib-homoprev.html#1948kinsey.

Kowalska, Monika. "The Heroines of My Life: Interview with Carys Massarella." *The Heroines of My Life*, April 13, 2014. http://theheroines.blogspot.ca/2014/04/interview-with-carys-massarella.html.

Kraehenbuhl, J. P. and M. R. Neutra. "Molecular and Cellular Basis of Immune Protection of Mucosal Surfaces." *Physiological Review* 72, no. 4 (October 1, 1992): 853–79.

Laurence, Lianne. "Judge Upholds Forced LGBT Indoctrination in Ontario Schools, Tells Christian Dad to Pull Kids out If He Objects | News | LifeSite." *LifeSiteNews*. November 24, 2016. https://www.lifesitenews.com/news/breaking-judge-upholds-forced-lgbt-indoctrination-in-ontario-schools-tells.

"Learning Activities: The Culture Connection." *ReCAPP: Resource Center for Adolescent Pregnancy Prevention*, copyright -2017 2007. http://recapp.etr.org/recapp/index.cfm?fuseaction=pages.LearningActivitiesDetail&pageID=160&PageTypeID=11.

Lees, Phil. "Kids in Northern Ontario School Told: 'Wear a Strap-on Penis.'" *PEACE Ontario Facebook Page*, September 26, 2015. https://www.facebook.com/PEACE-Ontario-358501781004633/timeline/.

Lees, Phil. "Sex Ed and Public Schools – Ontario: Guiding Through the Sex Ed Confusion." PEACE Ontario, 2015. http://peaceontario.com/wp-content/uploads/2015/01/PEACE-Sex-Ed-Report-2015.pdf.

Bibliography

"Lesbians and Birth Control," *Youth Resource,* accessed February 19, 2017, http://youthresource.com/health/women/index.htm

Logie, Carmen, "Queer Women are Ignored in HIV Research: This is a Problem and Here is Why it Matters," *CATIE Blog*, February 3, 2016, http://blog.catie.ca/2016/02/23/queer-women-are-ignored-in-hiv-research-this-is-a-problem-and-here-is-why-it-matters/

MacKellar, Duncan et al., "Unrecognized HIV infection, Risk Behaviors, and Perceptions of Risk among Young Men Who Have Sex with Men: Opportunities for Advancing HIV Prevention in the Third Decade of HIV/AIDS," *Journal of Acquired Immune Deficiency Syndromes* 38 no.5 (2005).

"Male Condoms and Sexually Transmitted Diseases." *U.S. Food & Drug Administration*, October 24, 2016. http://www.fda.gov/ForPatients/Illness/HIVAIDS/ucm126372.ht.

McGarry, Robert A., Lindsay Friedman, Teresa Bouley, and Pat Griffin. "Read, Set, Respect! GLSEN's Elementary School Toolkit." GLSEN, 2016. https://www.glsen.org/sites/default/files/GLSEN%20Ready%20Set%20Respect%202016.pdf.

McHugh, Paul. "Transgenderism: A Pathogenic Meme | Public Discourse." *The Witherspoon Institute: Public Discourse*, 2015. http://www.thepublicdiscourse.com/2015/06/15145/.

Mikkola, Mari. "Feminist Perspectives on Sex and Gender (Stanford Encyclopedia of Philosophy)." *Stanford Encyclopedia of Philosophy*, Spring 2016. https://plato.stanford.edu/entries/feminism-gender/#GenSocCon.

Ministry of Education. "Support for the Updated Health and Physical Education Curriculum." *Ontario Newsroom*, February 23, 2015. https://news.ontario.ca/edu/en/2015/02/support-for-the-updated-health-and-physical-education-curriculum.html.

Mitchell, Peter Jon. "Marriage: How Sticking with It Can Pay off." Archive of the Institute of Marriage and Family Canada (IMFC), August 12, 2015. http://www.imfcanada.org/archive/1094/marriage-how-sticking-it-can-pay.

"My GSA." *Egale: Canada Human Rights Trust*, 2015. http://egale.ca/portfolio/mygsa/.

Mykhalovskiy, E., Betteridge, Glen, and McLay, D. "HIV Non-Disclosure and the Criminal Law: Establishing Policy Options for Ontario. Toronto. A Report Funded by a Grant from the Ontario HIV Treatment Network." August 2010. http://www.catie.ca/pdf/Brochures/HIV-non-disclosure-criminal-law.pdf.

National Center for HIV/AIDS, Viral Hepatitis, STD, and TB Prevention. "CDC-Funded HIV Testing: United States, Puerto Rico, and the U.S. Virgin Islands, 2013." Centers for Disease Control and Prevention, 2013. https://www.cdc.gov/hiv/pdf/library/reports/cdc-hiv-CDCFunded_HIV_Testing_UnitedStates_Puerto_Rico_USVI_2013.pdf.

Nyhus, Nadine. "Opinion: Sex Ed Curriculum Inadequate and Should Be Withdrawn, Doctor Says." *Waterloo Region Record*. July 8, 2015.

http://www.therecord.com/opinion-story/5711922-opinion-sex-ed-curriculum-inadequate-and-should-be-withdrawn-doctor-says/.

"On This Day... Massachusetts Passes First Education Law." *Mass Moments*, copyright 2017. http://www.massmoments.org/moment.cfm?mid=113.

OnGov. "Sex Education in Ontario: Show of Hands." *Youtube*, September 10, 2015. https://www.youtube.com/watch?v=wamYCuBYzQ4&feature=youtu.be.

Ontario. Toronto. "Our Philosophy on Sexual Health." Toronto Public Health, copyright -2017 1998. http://www1.toronto.ca/wps/portal/contentonly?vgnextoid=adda0ab771790410VgnVCM10000071d60f89RCRD.

"Out Magazine - Gay & Lesbian Travel, Fashion & Culture." Accessed July 5, 2015. http://www.out.com/.

Parnell, Peter, and Justin Richardson. *And Tango Makes Three*. Simon & Schuster Children's Publishing, 2005.

Patel, Pragna, Craig B. Borkowf, John T. Brooks, Arielle Lasry, Amy Lansky, and Jonathan Mermin. "Estimating per-Act HIV Transmission Risk: A Systematic Review." *AIDS* 28, no. 10 (June 2014): 1509–19. doi:10.1097/QAD.0000000000000298.

"Persecution Against U.S. Christians On the Rise." *Samaritan's Purse*, April 30, 2015. https://www.samaritanspurse.org/article/persecution-against-u-s-christians-on-the-rise/.

Planned Parenthood Toronto. "Our Mission, Vision and Values." *Planned Parenthood Toronto*. Accessed January 26, 2017. http://www.ppt.on.ca/about-us/our-mission-vision-and-values/.

Ram, B. and F. Hou. "Changes in Family Structure and Child Outcomes: Roles of Economic and Familial Resources." *Policy Studies Journal* 31, no. 3 (2003): 317–19.

"Referral Database." *LGBT Youth Line*. Accessed August 24, 2015. http://www.youthline.ca/get-support/referral-database/.

Regenerus, Mark. "A Married Mom and Dad Really Do Matter: New Evidence from Canada." *The Witherspoon Institute: Public Discourse*, October 8, 2013. http://www.thepublicdiscourse.com/2013/10/10996/.

Reid, Jessica, David Hammond, and R Burkhalter. "Tobacco Use in Canada: Patterns and Trends, 2015 Edition." Propel Centre for Population Health Impact, University of Waterloo, 2015. http://tobaccoreport.ca/2015/TobaccoUseinCanada_2015.pdf.

"Respectfully Submitted: Policy Report for Parliamentarians." Association for Reformed Political Action Canada, Summer 2016. https://arpacanada.ca/wp-content/uploads/2016/07/Respectfully-Gender-Identity.pdf.

Rosin, Hanna. "A Boy's Life." *The Atlantic*, November 2008. https://www.theatlantic.com/magazine/archive/2008/11/a-boys-life/307059/.

"Same-Sex Couples and Sexual Orientation... by the Numbers." *Statistics Canada*, November 9, 2016. http://www.statcan.gc.ca/eng/dai/smr08/2015/smr08_203_2015.

Bibliography

Sandfort, Theo G. M. "Same-Sex Sexual Behavior and Psychiatric Disorders." *Archives of General Psychiatry (Journal of the American Medical Association)* 58, no. 1 (January 2001).

Savic, Ivanka, and Stefan Arver. "Sex Dimorphism of the Brain in Male-to-Female Transsexuals." *Oxford Journals*, 2015. http://cercor.oxfordjournals.org/content/early/2011/04/05/cercor.bhr032.full.

Schneider, Margaret, Walter O. Bocktin, Randall D. Ehrbar, Anne A. Lawrence, Katherine Louise Rachlin, and Kenneth J. Zucker. "Answers to Your Questions About Individuals With Intersex Conditions." American Psychological Association, 2006. https://www.apa.org/topics/lgbt/intersex.pdf.

"Sexual Activities." *Canadian Aids Society (Ottawa)*. Accessed November 4, 2015. http://www.cdnaids.ca/sexualactivities.

"Sexual Orientation." *KidsHealth*, 2017. http://kidshealth.org/en/parents/sexual-orientation.html.

Skutch, Robert. *Who's In A Family?* Tricycle Press, 1997.

Smith, Jessica. "Prominent Psychiatrist Speaks out against Conversion Therapy Legislation | Metro Toronto." *Toronto Metro*. March 30, 2015. http://www.metronews.ca/news/toronto/2015/03/30/prominent-psychiatrist-speaks-out-against-conversion-therapy-legislation.html.

Sterbenz, Christina. "The Words That Are Most Known to Only Men or Women." *Slate: Business Insider*, June 23, 2014. http://www.slate.com/blogs/business_insider/2014/06/23/center_for_reading_research_study_finds_different_vocabulary_words_are_known.html.

Stone, Dan. "The Bigger Brains of London Taxi Drivers." *National Geographic Magazine*, May 29, 2013. http://voices.nationalgeographic.com/2013/05/29/the-bigger-brains-of-london-taxi-drivers/.

"Stories," Living Out, accessed January 31, http://www.livingout.org/stories

Strachan, Owen. "Transgender Identity—Wishing Away God's Design." *Answers in Genesis*, July 24, 2016. https://answersingenesis.org/family/gender/transgender-identity-wishing-away-gods-design/?utm_source=facebook-aig&utm_medium=social&utm_content=transgenderidentitywishingawaygodsdesign-19789&utm_campaign=20150416.

"Suggestions for Writing about Intersex | Intersex Society of North America." *Intersex Society of North America*, 2008. http://www.isna.org/node/977.

"Swell of Same-Sex Families Ushering in 'the New Normal' - Montreal - CBC News." *CBC News, Montreal*, November 9, 2012. http://www.cbc.ca/news/canada/montreal/swell-of-same-sex-families-ushering-in-the-new-normal-1.1204886.

"Terminology." *Gender Diversity*, 2016. http://www.genderdiversity.org/resources/terminology/.

The Associated Press. "David Reimer, 38, Subject of the John/Joan Case." *The New York Times*, May 12, 2004. http://www.nytimes.com/2004/05/12/us/david-reimer-38-subject-of-the-john-joan-case.html?_r=1.

The Canadian Press. "Justin Trudeau at Pride Toronto: 'We Can't Let Hate Go By'." *Macleans*. Accessed January 25, 2017. http://www.macleans.ca/news/canada/justin-trudeau-at-pride-toronto-we-cant-let-hate-go-by/.

Thomas, R. K. and Bartelli, D. "HIV Services for a New Generation. - PubMed - NCBI." *Marketing Health Services* 21, no. 4 (January 2001): 24–29.

"TIMELINE | Same-Sex Rights in Canada - Canada - CBC News." News. *CBCNews*, May 25, 2015. http://www.cbc.ca/news/canada/timeline-same-sex-rights-in-canada-1.1147516.

"Tracking the Hidden Epidemics, Trends in STDs in the United States (2000)." Centers for Disease Control and Prevention, 2000. https://www.cdc.gov/std/trends2000/trends2000.pdf.

"Trinity Western Law School Decision Overturned by B.C. Supreme Court - British Columbia - CBC News." *CBCNews*, December 10, 2015. http://www.cbc.ca/news/canada/british-columbia/trinity-western-law-society-bc-supreme-court-1.3359942.

Ubelacker, Sheryl. "Group Protests Closure of Youth Gender Identity Clinic at CAMH, Director's Removal." *Global News*, January 23, 2016. http://globalnews.ca/news/2473568/group-protests-closure-of-youth-gender-identity-clinic-at-camh-directors-removal/.

Victoros, Helen, Kelly Hayes, and Izida Zorde. "Creating Safe and Inclusive Schools for Gender Independent Children: Interview with Dr. Carys Massarella." *ETFO Voice*, Summer 2012.

Vitale, Anne. "Guilt and Shame: The Unfortunate Twins of Gender Dysphoria." *Avitale.com*, October 12, 1996. http://www.avitale.com/GuiltShame.htm.

Vivio, Lavern. "I Wished I Had Been Born a Boy | Uturnlavern's Blog." *Uturnlavern's Blog: Thoughts and Opinions from Uturn Lavern*, June 4, 2015. https://uturnlavern.wordpress.com/2015/06/04/155/.

Walsh, Matt. "Forcing Girls To Share A Bathroom With A Gender-Confused Boy Is Abuse – TheBlaze," September 2, 2015. http://www.theblaze.com/contributions/forcing-girls-to-share-a-bathroom-with-a-gender-confused-boy-is-abuse/.

Weatherbe, Steve. "Trudeau Promises to Decriminalize Anal Sex for 16-Year-Olds." *LifeSiteNews*. July 6, 2016. https://www.lifesitenews.com/news/trudeau-promises-to-decriminalize-anal-sex-for-16-year-olds.

"Welcoming and Supporting Lesbian, Gay, Bisexual, and Transgender Families." Elementary Teachers' Federation of Ontario. Accessed June 17, 2015. http://www.etfo.ca/Resources/LGBTfamilies/Documents/SupportingLGBTFamilies%20.pdf.

Wells, Kristopher, Gayle Roberts, and Carol Allan. "Supporting Transgender and Transsexual Students in K-12 Schools: A Guide for Educators." Canadian Teachers' Federation, Ottawa, Ontario, 2012. http://gendercreativekids.ca/wp-content/uploads/2013/10/Supporting-Transgender-and-Transsexual-Students-web.pdf.

Bibliography

Wente, Margaret. "Transgender Kids: Have We Gone Too Far? - The Globe and Mail." *The Globe and Mail*. February 15, 2014. http://www.theglobeandmail.com/opinion/transgender-kids-have-we-gone-too-far/article16897043/.

"'Who's in a Family?' - in the Diversity Book Bag." *Mass Resistance*. Accessed January 26, 2017. http://www.massresistance.org/docs/parker/diversity_book.html.

Wilton, James. "STIs: What Role Do They Play in HIV Transmission?" *CATIE - Canada's Source for HIV and Hepatitis C Information*, Spring 2012. http://www.catie.ca/en/pif/spring-2012/stis-what-role-do-they-play-hiv-transmission.

Woods, Mark. "Transgender and Christian: How Caitlyn Jenner Challenges the Church." *Christian Today*, June 3, 2015. http://www.christiantoday.com/article/transgender.and.christian.how.caitlyn.jenner.challenges.the.church/55334.htm.

Zhou, Jiang-Ning, Michel A. Hofman, Louis J. G. Gooren, and Dick F. Swaab. "A Sex Difference in the Human Brain and Its Relation to Transsexuality." *Nature Publishing Group* 378 (November 1995): 68–70. doi:10.1038/378068a0.

Zwibel, Cara Faith. "Faith in the Public School System: Principles for Reconciliation | Ontario Human Rights Commission." *Creed, Freedom of Religion and Human Rights - Special Issue of Diversity Magazine*, Summer 2012. http://www.ohrc.on.ca/sites/default/files/Diversity%20Magazine_Creed_freedom%20of%20religion-human%20rights_accessible.pdf.

GLOSSARY

The provision of the definitions below is to establish the meaning of the terms as presently understood by our culture and as used in this book.

AIDS (Acquired Immune Deficiency Syndrome): HIV (Human Immunodeficiency Virus) can lead to AIDS, a state of health in which a person's immune system has been weakened by HIV and the person can no longer fight other infections. It is common for a person with AIDS to develop other infections, such as pneumonia or some kinds of cancer. See also HIV.[1]

Bisexual: A person who is emotionally/romantically/sexually/physically attracted to and/or involved with both men and women.[2]

Expectation: The curriculum expectations (overall and specific expectations) are the knowledge and skills that students are expected to demonstrate in each subject at each grade level by the end of the grade.

Felt Gender: The gender a trans person feels themselves to be – the opposite gender or the 'Felt Gender'.[3]

Gender: A term that refers to those characteristics of women and men that are socially constructed.[4]

Gender Expression: The manner in which individuals express their gender identity to others. A person's gender expression is often based on a social construct of gender, which is either stereotypically male or female. However, some individuals who do not see themselves as being either male or female but as some combination of the two genders, or as without gender, choose to express their identity in terms of a multiple model of gender, mixing both male and female expressions.[5]

Gender Identity: A person's sense of self, with respect to being male or female. Gender identity is different from sexual orientation and may be different from birth-assigned sex.[6]

Heterosexism: The social, systemic, and personal assumptions, practices, and behaviours that assume that heterosexuality is the only natural and acceptable sexual orientation. [7]

HIV (Human Immunodeficiency Virus): A serious viral infection that can be controlled with treatments. HIV attacks the cells in the body that help to fight infections until they are no longer able to do their job. With treatment, the damage that HIV does to the body's immune system can be slowed or prevented. But HIV infection cannot be cured. The only way to know if you have HIV is to get an HIV test. Today, when people get tested for HIV early in the infection and access HIV treatments, they have the opportunity to live a near-to-normal lifespan. HIV can lead to AIDS (see also AIDS). [8]

Homophobia: A disparaging or hostile attitude or a negative bias, which may be overt or unspoken and which may exist at an individual and/or a systemic level, towards people who are lesbian, gay, bisexual, or transgender (LGBT). [9]

Indoctrination: To teach (someone) to fully accept the ideas, opinions, and beliefs of a particular group and to not consider other ideas, opinions, and beliefs. [10]

Intersex: A term used to describe a person whose sex chromosomes, genitalia, and/or secondary sex characteristics (e.g., facial hair, breasts) are determined to be neither exclusively male nor female. An intersex person may have biological characteristics of both the male and female sexes. The intersex community has generally rejected the term "hermaphrodite" as outdated. Intersex people may or may not identify as part of the transgender community. See also gender identity, transgender, and transsexual. [11]

Pansexual: a person who experiences sexual, romantic, physical, and/or spiritual attraction for members of all gender identities/expressions. Often shortened to "pan." [12]

Same-sex Attraction: Someone who sometimes experiences sexual attraction to the same sex but does not assume a homosexual identity. [13]

Sex: The category of male or female based on characteristics that are biologically determined.[14]

Sexual Identification: Choosing to identify as a homosexual or heterosexual person; the acknowledgement that one is straight or gay/lesbian; distinct from same-sex attraction.[15]

Sexual Orientation: A person's sense of sexual attraction to people of the same sex, the opposite sex, or both sexes.[16]

Stereotype: A false or generalized, and usually negative, conception of a group of people that results in the unconscious or conscious categorization of each member of that group, without regard for individual differences. Stereotyping may be based on race, ancestry, place of origin, colour, ethnic origin, citizenship, creed, sex, sexual orientation, age, marital status, family status, or disability, as set out in the Ontario Human Rights Code, or on the basis of other factors.[17]

Transgender: A transgender person is a person whose gender identity, outward appearance, gender expression, and/or anatomy are not consistent with the conventional definitions or expectations of male and female; often used to represent a wide range of gender identities and behaviours.[18]

Transmale: A person who was assigned a female sex at birth but identifies as a man.[19]

Transfemale: A person who was assigned a male sex at birth but identifies as a woman.[20]

Transsexual: A person who experiences intense personal and emotional discomfort with his or her assigned birth gender and may undergo treatment to transition gender.[21]

Two-spirited: A term used by First Nations people to refer to a person having both the feminine and masculine spirits. It includes sexual or gender identity, sexual orientation, social roles, and a broad range of identities, such as lesbian, gay, bisexual, and transgender.[22]

[1] Ontario, Ministry of Education, *The Ontario Curriculum, Grades 1-8: Health and Physical Education*, 197.
[2] Ibid., 228
[3] "Gender Definitions," *Trans-Parenting*, accessed January 27, 2017, http://www.trans-parenting.com/understanding-gender/gender-definitions/.
[4] Ontario, Ministry of Education, *The Ontario Curriculum, Grades 1-8: Health and Physical Education*, 231.
[5] Ibid.
[6] Ibid.
[7] Ast et al., *Challenging Homophobia and Heterosexism*, 209.
[8] Ontario, Ministry of Education, *The Ontario Curriculum, Grades 1-8: Health and Physical Education*, 197.
[9] Ibid., 232.
[10] "Indoctrinate," *Merriam-Webster*, 2017, https://www.merriam-webster.com/dictionary/indoctrinate.
[11] Ontario, Ministry of Education, *The Ontario Curriculum, Grades 1-8: Health and Physical Education*, 232.
[12] Sam Killerman, "Comprehensive* List of LGBTQ+ Vocabulary Definitions," *It's Pronounced METROsexual*, accessed January 27, 2017, http://itspronouncedmetrosexual.com/2013/01/a-comprehensive-list-of-lgbtq-term-definitions/#sthash.lofZmUJM.dpbs.
[13] Definition developed by authors.
[14] Ontario, Ministry of Education, *The Ontario Curriculum, Grades 9-12: Health and Physical Education*, 216.
[15] Definition developed by authors.
[16] Ontario, Ministry of Education, *The Ontario Curriculum, Grades 1-8: Health and Physical Education*, 236.
[17] Ibid., 237.
[18] Ibid., 239.
[19] Killerman, "Comprehensive* List of LGBTQ+ Vocabulary Definitions."
[20] Ibid.
[21] Ontario, Ministry of Education, *The Ontario Curriculum, Grades 1-8: Health and Physical Education*, 239.
[22] Ibid., 239.

INDEX

A ~
abstinence, 190-194
AIDS, 130, 178, 179, 187, 190
anal cancer, 183, 188
anal sex, 181-188, 191

B ~
barriers to acceptance of gender identity and sexual orientation, 125-129
Bill 13, *"The Accepting Schools Act"*, 32
Bill 77, *"Affirming Sexual Orientaiton and Gender Identity Act 2015"*, 56-57
Bradley, Dr. Susan, 55, 56

C ~
Canadian AIDS Society, 130-131, 189
Canadian Teachers' Federation, 141
Challenging Homophobia and Heterosexism, 31, 122, 145, 156
compromise, 19-21
condoms, 178-182
cultural values, 165-170
Curve Magazine, 147

E ~
Elementary Teachers' Federation of Ontario (ETFO), 126, 156
Evangelical Fellowship of Canada (EFC), 112-115, 192

F ~
family values, 124, 165-170, 202
feminity/masculinity spectrum, 87-93

G ~
gay rights, 27-30
gay-straight alliance (GSA), 128, 170, 172-174, 216
gender dysphoria, 27, 51-57, 83, 95
Genderbread person, 47-49, 78, 87
goal of sex ed curriculum, 129-131

H ~
heterosexism, 105-106, 122-123, 131, 216
HIV, 26, 130-131, 178-190, 194, 214

homophobia, 14, 26, 27, 31, 35, 37, 99, 103, 105, 122-125, 127, 130, 137, 156, 166, 201-202, 215-216
Human papillomavirus (HPV), 180, 183

I ~
identity, 62-70
intersex, 47, 51-52, 127

J ~
Jealousy, 80-83
John/Joan, 135-136

K ~
Kids Help Phone, 105, 171
Kinsey, Dr. Alfred (also: "Kinsey Report"), 28, 29, 42

L ~
Lady Gaga, 43-44
LGBT Youth Line, 171-172
Lie-dentity, 47, 69-70, 73-74, 77-78

M ~
masculinity/feminity spectrum, 87-93
Massarella, Dr. Carys, 53, 56
media, 19, 62, 99, 127, 132, 156, 166, 201-202
barrier of media, 144-148

milestones in accepting an LGB identity, 46, 206
Money, Dr. John, 135

O ~
Ontario Curriculum
Arts, 31, 125, 126
Language, 31, 157
Social Studies, 32, 153, 157, 212, 216
Ontario Human Rights Code ("the Code"), 28-31, 107-110, 112, 166
OPHEA, 144, 145, 168, 179, 108
Out Magazine, 147

P ~
pansexualism, 42, 205
Policy/Program Memorandum No. 145: *Progressive Discipline and Promoting Positive Student Behaviour*, 32, 104, 105, 171
parental rights, 112-116

R ~
religious freedom, 103-116
religious values, 165-170

S ~

same-sex attraction, 27, 45-47, 66, 72
same-sex families/marriage, 28-29, 132, 151-160
self-awareness, 57, 127, 132, 166, 200-205
self-concept, 137, 166, 203-207
self-harm, 2, 51, 140
sexual identification, 69-73
sexually transmitted infections (STIs), 178-194
    chlamydia, 180, 188
    genital herpes, 180
    gonorrhea, 180, 188
    HPV, 180, 183
    syphilis, 180, 188
    trichomonas, 180
Skutch, Robert, 156-157
social justice, 122-125
stereotypes, 31, 87, 95, 97, 99, 125, 135-148
stigma, 127, 166, 178, 189-190
    re. HIV, 187-190

suicide, 26, 27, 32, 48, 136, 140, 172

T ~

telephone help lines, 105, 165, 171
Toronto District School Board (TDSB), 25, 31, 106, 122, 145, 156
transgender rights, 27-29
transphobia, 26, 107, 130, 156
two-spirited, 47, 127, 139, 140, 145, 174, 201

X ~

Xtra Magazine, 147

Z ~

Zucker, Dr. Kenneth, 51, 56, 57

Made in the USA
Columbia, SC
16 November 2017